Party Man, Company Man:
Is China's State Capitalism Doomed?

Joe Zhang

Enrich Professional Publishing

Honolulu • Hong Kong • Beijing • Singapore

Published by

Enrich Professional Publishing, Inc.
Suite 208
Davies Pacific Center
841 Bishop Street
Honolulu, HI, 96813
Website: www.enrichprofessional.com
A Member of Enrich Culture Group Limited

Hong Kong Head Office:
11/F, Benson Tower, 74 Hung To Road, Kwun Tong, Kowloon,
Hong Kong, China

China Office:
Rm 309, Building A, Central Valley, 16 Hai Dian Zhong Jie, Haidian District,
Beijing, China

Singapore Office:
16L, Enterprise Road, Singapore 627660

English edition © 2014 by Enrich Professional Publishing, Inc.

Edited by Glenn Griffith and Vivian C. W. Hui

ISBN (Paperback)   978-1-62320-038-1
ISBN (ebook)   978-1-62320-057-2

Enrich Professional Publishing is an independent globally-minded publisher
focusing on the economic and financial developments that have revolutionized
New China. We aim to serve the needs of advanced degree students,
researchers, and business professionals who are looking for authoritative,
accurate, and engaging information on China.

This publication is designed to provide accurate and authoritative information
in regard to the subject matter covered. It is sold with the understanding
that the publisher is not engaged in rendering legal, accounting, or other
professional services. If legal advice or other expert assistance is required, the
services of a competent professional person should be sought.

This book is based on facts and the author's understanding of the facts. It
has been written in good faith. In several cases, names have been hidden or
masked in order to avoid embarrassment for the persons involved.

Investment is a risky game, and neither the author nor the publisher will
accept any responsibility for losses as a result of reading this book or acting
on its views.

Printed in Hong Kong.

Dedicated to

Hu Aimin and Zhang Yijun,

former Chairman and former CEO of

Shenzhen Investment, respectively,

who taught me that the state sector was

more than just dollars and cents.

Contents

Foreword

Deflating China's Credit Bubble

For a company with, say, one million shares, increasing the number of shares to two million will simply dilute the underlying value of each share by exactly a half. But for a country, it works differently.

The purest form of monetarism would say that increasing (or decreasing) the amount of money in the economy does not affect the way the economy works. In other words, the change in the amount of money in circulation will automatically be spread equally among all the participants of the economy.

Sadly, the economy does not work like a corporate, even in the long run. The fact that pump-priming is still adopted by many governments means it remains effective. The quantitative easing (QE) pursued by the U.S. and Europe in the aftermath of the global financial crisis in 2008 is a classic form of pump-priming. Has it worked? It depends on your definition of "working." I think it has worked quite well. While it has not changed these countries' underlying growth potential, it has achieved two objectives. First, it has calmed the capital markets and prevented panic from spreading.

Second, it has made the banks real again. Following the financial crisis of 2008 there was the sudden realization that many banks in the Western world had too much debt and the sharp decline of asset values meant that many (and probably most) banks were either broke (technically insolvent) or were left with very thin net worth.

How did the central banks rescue them? The central banks lent almost unlimited amounts of money to the banks (at, say, 1% to 2% per annum) and the banks then invested the money in bonds (at say, 3% to 4%) and loans (at 5% to 6%). The yield gap was the single most important reason (if not the only reason) why the banks have been alive and kicking again since 2011. The big bonuses for bankers have staged a comeback since 2012.

In this book, I have not tried to rigorously prove whether pump-priming works in general. But the experience in the U.S. and Europe since 2008 can prove that it works at least some of the time.

In China, the inflationary policy of the past 35 years (since Deng Xiaoping came to power in 1978) has worked extremely effectively, for two extra reasons. First, the transformation in the countryside (from collective farming in the form of communes to family-based garden-style farming) sharply increased productivity, and released hundreds of millions of cheap workers to the manufacturing and service sectors. Marrying the fresh credit from the banks with cheap labor has done wonders to China's factories.

Second, the bulk of the economy was and still is controlled by the state. The SOEs are less sensitive to interest rates, and more sensitive to the availability of funds. Many do not care much about the returns on their bank credit, and in some cases, not even the returns of their bank credit. They are more interested in expanding their output (and thus power base). Their carefree way of investing (or spending) has boosted economic activities as a result.

In the meantime, official controls over interest rates have amounted to a subsidy to borrowers, encouraging the private sector as well as the state sector to borrow more to invest.

A Self-Fulfilling Prophecy

It has become a self-fulfilling prophecy: increasing the amount of fiat money (in the form of bank credit) in the economy has boosted economic output, and the prices of products and input (such as labor, raw materials, and machines). Higher prices of products and input, in turn, demand more credit just to lubricate the functioning of the same amount of production. To increase the production in real terms (i.e., in quantity terms), requires still more bank credit. Once this modus operandi is in place, the rest, as they say, is history.

Now, after 35 years of the high growth of economic activity and of money supply, prices (of everything) have gone up substantially. As a consequence, the stimulus power of money (and bank credit) has diminished. To achieve the same impact on economic output, a higher dose of monetary stimulus is required.

The Chinese government and the public have taken the high growth of output for granted just when the negative consequences of credit expansion start to hurt: industrial overcapacity, weak returns on invested capital, environmental destruction, and income disparity.

China's Readiness to Intervene

In hindsight, the global financial crisis in the U.S. from 2007 to 2008 was directly caused (or at least worsened) by the free-market religion long pursued by the U.S. government and the U.S. Federal Reserve. Was the crisis really inevitable? Not really. If the Fed and the U.S. government had poured money at Lehman Brothers, Merrill Lynch, and all the other "too big to fail" institutions when the first sign of panic emerged, there would not have been a global crisis. In my view, it is their religion and the institutional constraints (the budget restrictions the U.S. Congress had placed on the executive branch of the government, and the political bickering in the Congress) that made a long-term structural decay in the U.S. and European economies an explosive crisis.

In China, there would not have been Congressional debates or executive hesitation in the event of such a crisis. They would just do it, the same way the 4 trillion yuan of stimulus package was doled out in late 2008 and early 2009 when the U.S. congressional leaders were locked in debates.

After much politicking, the U.S. government and the Fed did pretty much what the Chinese government would have done straight away. The only difference was they did so grudgingly, reluctantly, and belatedly. The meeting minutes of the U.S. Federal Reserve Board in 2007 and 2008 released in early 2014 showed that, apart from a religious aversion to intervention, there was also a major misjudgment on the part of the Federal Reserve on the scale of the crisis in 2007 to 2008.

In 2013, the assault by China's shadow banking activities and the internet on traditional banks gained momentum. Through online fund-raising (at higher interest rates) and the offers of wealth management products, shadow bankers achieved massive popularity, pushed up market interest rates, and diverted sizable funds away from the banks — soon forcing the banks to match their high interest rates.

The official controls over the interest rates on bank deposits seemed to be crumbling in late 2013 and early 2014. In response, Zhou Xiaochuan, the Governor of the People's Bank of China, promised in March 2014 to remove the controls on interest rates "within a year or two." It is not clear if the government will keep this promise (as many other promises have been broken without an apology or even explanation). As I noted in my book, *Inside China's Shadow Banking: The Next Subprime Crisis?*, the central bank has promised "interest rate liberalization within five years" since 1986. But the five years have never arrived. I hope the new target of "a year or two" will arrive sooner.

Since 2012 or 2013, a gradual increase of market interest rates and tightening of bank credit reinforced a slowdown in the economy. Some shadow banking products (trusts) and highly-geared borrowers started to default, at a time real estate prices started to soften and sales volumes slowed.

Gentle Deflation of the Bubble

Is this a prelude to the bursting of China's credit bubble and real estate bubble? I think not.

I think the most likely scenario is a gradual deflating of the bubbles over a 3-to-5-year period. Maybe even longer.

But is China able to prevent a dramatic burst of the bubbles, you may ask. I think it is, for several reasons.

First of all, unlike the U.S. or Europe, there are very few financial derivatives in China today. That means that a financial contagion is likely to be less rapid and less damaging.

Second, the Chinese household sector is very under-geared. Credit card debts are a tiny fraction (low single-digits) of the banking industry assets. Student loans are virtually non-existent. Auto loans are negligible. Mortgage loans on housing have grown big but nothing like in the U.S. or Europe. For most mortgages, the real estate prices would have to fall one-third or even half before hitting equity values. The maximum loan-to-value ratios are 80% for first home buyers, and 30% for buyers of second and third homes. Most mortgages (even those on first-homes) older than a few years have built a thick cushion on the back of two factors: steady repayment, and rising property prices. In the whole country, there are few reverse mortgages (or home equity loans). Second mortgages provided by developers are rare. Even rarer are teaser loans (or adjustable rate mortgages) and interest-only loans seen in the U.S. Mortgage-backed securitization is an alien concept to China, therefore, lenders do not have the in-built incentive to lend to those deemed unable to repay. After all, the originators of mortgages cannot engage in a fraudulent practice of "lend and flip." At the macro policy level, while it is the government's monetary policy and interest rate controls that have fuelled the property bubble, the government has been downright hostile to the real estate sector since 2009 to 2010.

Third, corporate leverage is high in China, but again, two-thirds of the economy is still wholly or partly owned by the state. The government currently runs a broadly balanced budget. Despite accumulated debts that are said to be over 50% of GDP, one must also consider the government's vast assets (including foreign-currency assets) and cash flows. At a practical level, the central government and the six layers of local governments are one and the same thing. The central government not only dictates local governments' taxes and expenditures, but also dictates its revenue-sharing formula with each local government. In many cases, the central government also issues bonds on behalf of the local governments — proof that local governments are simply "subsidiaries" of the central government. You are unlikely to see Detroit or Orange County go bust while the central government stands idly by. Indeed, take note of the terminology here: we use the term "the central government", rather than "the federal government."

At present, we have seen no pressure for the central or even local governments to offload assets in order to repay their debts. We are not there yet. And I think we are far from it. There is ample scope for the government to kick the can of debts further down the road.

Lessons from the Stock Market

It is interesting to draw inspiration from the deflation of China's stock market bubble in the past 22 years. Yes, 22 years! Almost since that market was created in 1992, it has been a bubble. Since then, the price-earnings multiples in the market have fallen from around 100 times initially to around 20 times in 2013 to 2014. The 16 listed banks currently trade at much lower (single-digit) multiples, and drag the market average of multiples down. Excluding the banks, however, the domestic stock market is still on 20-odd times, and deflating still.

The stock market deflation has destroyed trillions of yuan of financial worth, and hurt millions of innocent savers and gamblers alike — over 22 years. The agony is well-known. In these 22 years, the country's money supply has grown an accumulative 43.5 times, but the stock market is still gasping for air. It is truly a water torture. The government has tried all sorts of tactics to stop the misery, but only to be humiliated repeatedly.

Finally, some cultural or institutional factors may support my benign prediction of a gradual deflation of the bubbles. For example, a strange phenomenon in the Chinese mutual fund industry is that retail (and even corporate) investors would always sell their investments in well-performing funds, while tightly holding on to their units in poorly-performing and underwater funds. They have a way to describe their behavior: "I am only stuck, and I am not losing money if I do not sell."

Irrational? Maybe. Peter Lynch, the famous Boston-based fund manager who used to manage money at Fidelity, ridiculed this behavior as "pulling the flowers and watering the weeds."

So, just as they behave in the stock market, Chinese retail investors, instead of bailing out of a weakening real estate market, will most likely hold tightly onto their holdings of housing units if the prices should weaken, provided they have the holding power — and macro data suggests that they do. In my view, that will be an important automatic stabilizer to the market.

But what if they all rush to the exit? Of course, the real estate prices will collapse as a result. But it is important to remember these facts:

1. Unlike the U.S., Chinese persons or households cannot declare bankruptcy or walk away from their mortgages. In other words, their mortgage liabilities will be with them forever, until fully repaid. That is a disincentive for borrowers to walk away.

2. The borrowers have a strong incentive to keep their credit ratings. The stigma attached to housing defaults is severe. In Hong Kong, for example, where persons can declare bankruptcy, hundreds of thousands of households have continued to service their mortgages, for over a decade, after the values of their housing units had fallen well below their mortgage liabilities since the Asian Financial Crisis in 1997. Even in 2013 to 2014 (i.e., 15 years later), tens of thousands of housing units are still under water (the local term is "negative equity"), and these households are still repaying their loans month after month.

So, what is going to happen to the millions of vacant housing units, and the crazy housing prices across China? The outcome is most likely a gradual deflation, lasting many years.

In March 2014, Jin Liqun, CEO of China Investment Corp, the country's sovereign wealth fund, noted in *Caijing*, the burden of the real estate bubble will ultimately be borne by the households. I agree. I think that the millions of vacant housing units and the deflation of their value will constitute a destruction of household savings and wealth, much the same as the protracted deflation of the country's stock market. This should have a "wealth effect" on the economy: consumers think they have extra savings in the form of an apartment somewhere, but the apartment neither negates cash flows nor has any durability. But as the realization of the destruction of wealth (and savings) is spread out among hundreds of millions of savers over many years, its drag on the economy is gradual rather than dramatic.

Introduction

While only 51 years old, I feel that I have lived several lifetimes. I've gone from the rural landscape of central China to the central bank in Beijing, and then to school for six years in Australia, and then on to the quick-buck world of investment banking in Hong Kong, microfinance in Guangzhou, and now the private sector advisory business. To me, things have just moved too fast. I have hardly had time to reflect. If my first book published last year, *Inside China's Shadow Banking: The Next Subprime Crisis?*, was a memoir of my experience as an economic outsider fighting against the state capitalist regime, this book is about my time as an insider running a favored government business.

In early 2006, when I was offered the job of Chief Operating Officer (COO) by Shenzhen Investment Limited, a state-controlled company listed on the Hong Kong Stock Exchange, it came to my mind all the stock options and big bucks I was going to make. After all, this state-owned enterprise (SOE) was a prime candidate for turnaround. Although its market value was only 400 million U.S. dollars, it had some good assets, including prime real estate, and stakes in a big power plant, cable TV operations, and profitable factories.

I joked to a friend of mine, "With a lot of low-hanging fruit, my turn to make a quick buck has just arrived. Who says that only American corporate executives are entitled to fat gains on stock options?"

But I left the company six months before my three-year contract had run out. I had underestimated the difficulties of reforms in an established and entrenched SOE. In those three years, I also sat on the boards of directors of two other companies, also controlled by the state: Shenzhen International and Guangzhou Investment. I have learned a thing or two on how the Communist Party manages the state sector. Equally, I have seen how its approach to business management has evolved since then.

A Policy Reversal

"China's state sector is corrupt, inefficient and ideologically inferior; so, they must be losing the battle against private sector capitalism, left, right, and center." That is the conventional liberal view. The argument is neat. Sadly, however, it is not true — particularly the second part of the argument.

There are indeed many problems facing the state sector in China. Some of the problems may even be incurable. But they are rarely fatal.

To be fair, China's state sector is constantly adapting to public demand for more transparency, and higher efficiency. It is not only surviving, but also prospering. In the past decade, the state sector has regained economic prominence. In fact, China has undone most of the economic liberalization that was achieved in the previous two decades.

Importantly, this has not taken place against the public's wishes. I think the public wants an even bigger state sector and a more effective and more assertive government. In light of the four biggest challenges China faces — namely, inequality, the environmental crisis, the depletion of resources, and overpopulation — the public is demanding more, not less, involvement by the state.

Given the global shift of views on state capitalism, along with China's unique set of challenges, I believe that the state sector will become much more prominent in China in the next few decades.

The Chinese public's bias against private sector capitalism is deep-rooted. No wonder there is systematic discrimination against the private sector. In the awarding of government contracts, bureaucrats' self-censorship hurts private sector bidders. In the banking sector, risk-averse credit officers tend to avoid borrowers from the private sector. In most of the past 35 years, China's interest rates have been below inflation, and as a result, a huge amount of subsidies are embedded in the loan.

Unfortunately, the credit rationing process is heavily skewed against the private sector. In fact, there are two credit markets: one for the state sector and a small number of privileged private sector entrepreneurs, and the other is for the vast majority of the private sector. In the first credit market, lending rates range from 6% to 8% a year, while in the second credit market, interest rates typically span 10% to 30% — if you can get a credit ration at all. The operators of the second credit market are shadow banks such as trust companies, finance companies, microcredit firms, pawnshops, junk bonds, and the banks' wealth management products.

To escape discrimination, and in pursuit of equal opportunity, a large number of private businesses have unfortunately resorted to corruption and violation of the rules, reinforcing the public's prejudice that the private sector is not to be trusted. It is a vicious circle. Many entrepreneurs have become part-time politicians in search of political protection, and favors. While their political presence is mostly constructive to the well-being of society, there are unintended consequences: The mixing of politics with business has cemented the private sector's status as being only a supplement to the state sector, instead of an equal force.

Even without the cultural undercurrents unique to China, the private sector has its fair share of problems. China's private sector is vulnerable as it suffers from diseconomies of scale. A volatile business environment calls for diversification but small businesses do not always have the luxury to diversify. Each year, tens of thousands of private sector businesses go bankrupt or are forced to close shop because of turbulence in the economy, their own mismanagement, as well as systematic discrimination against them. Those who claim the private sector is winning the battle against the state sector have confused wishful thinking with reality.

The Way Forward

In this book, I try not to enter the debate as to whether or not private sector capitalism is superior to state capitalism. There are countless books on that topic, and I do not think I can add much to the debate. So, I focus on my real experience at the three SOEs (mainly Shenzhen Investment), and my views on what the Chinese public wants. In other words, I focus on how state capitalism *will* evolve in China, rather than how it *should* evolve. My conclusion is that the state sector, for good or bad, will become far more intrusive and pervasive in China in the next few decades.

I have a few unanswered questions: Is the dominant state sector crowding out private investments, or creating markets for the private sector? What role, if any, does China's state sector play in the imbalances of the economy? Is the fast-growing state sector likely to prolong the imbalances? Is China's rapid growth of the past 35 years the triumph of Keynesian economics?

The book is organized as follows: the first nine chapters chronicle my experiences while running a reasonably big business, as well as my frustration at dealing with the inefficiency and corruption that is common in the state sector. I highlight some critical make-or-break parts of the life of a company, namely acquisitions and the disposal of major assets.

In the next eight chapters of the book, I answer the question: Why has state sector reform in China gone backward, instead of forward, in the past decade? I analyze why this inconvenient truth is largely ignored by Western observers, while it is widely accepted as a fact inside China. It is true that the government has sold off a big number of enterprises in the past three decades, but that has only relieved the government of a huge financial and political burden. By holding tightly onto strategically important sectors, such as infrastructure, telecoms, banking, finance, and tobacco, the government has not only turned itself into the Warren Buffett of China, but it also retains the maximum financial flexibility of a broadly balanced budget and the ability to pick winners where it sees them.

1
Chapter

Jumping Ship to Canada: A Senior Manager Flees

PARTY MAN, COMPANY MAN

In May 2007, as I took the podium to address 40 senior and mid-level executives of Shenzhen Investment Limited, my mind flashed back to a few months earlier. The memory of one executive's spectacular escape was going a long way towards distracting me from my nervousness about the speech I was about to give.

At 2 on a cold Sunday morning in February 2007, the phone rang and I bolted upright. I was at a ski resort in Zhangjiakou, three hours by car north of Beijing, on a mini-vacation. On the line was my boss, Hu Aimin, Chairman of Shenzhen Investment Limited, a government-controlled conglomerate company listed on the Hong Kong Stock Exchange. I was the company's Chief Operating Officer and a board member. This was my first vacation after taking the job nearly a year earlier. When I had gone to bed Saturday night I had no idea that my Sunday was going to start so early and with so much drama.

Hu sounded very tired and a bit depressed and he was coughing badly.

"Let me guess: an accident on our construction site?" I quipped. Two years earlier, a digger at one of our sites hurt a nearby pedestrian and, understandably, the whole management team had been nervous about casualties ever since.

"Just as bad," came the reply. Lin Minrui, the head of Dafu Corporation based in Zhuhai, one of the major subsidiaries of Shenzhen Investment, had just fled to Canada apparently because he was afraid that he was going to be arrested by the Communist Party Disciplinary Committee of Zhuhai City! Lin, 55, had held that position at Dafu for over five years, and Dafu had been a net drag on the larger group's overall financial performance.

"My God. I had indeed expected something like this," I said.

"Can you please come back to Hong Kong to deal with this?" Hu asked.

I started packing my bags again. The vacation was over. On the previous Thursday, the Disciplinary Committee had called Lin in for "coffee" at 2 in the afternoon. He panicked and wasted no time to rush to Hong Kong where he booked the first available flight to Vancouver. The Disciplinary Committee's call in the morning had apparently given everything away as the appointment for coffee was at Pengfulou Hotel. That was the spot where quite a few officials had been arrested for corruption and a host of other misdeeds. Consequently, the hotel had been given the nickname "The Bermuda Hotel" by some civil servants in China, a nod to the famous Bermuda Triangle where planes and ships had disappeared.

When Lin had failed to show up for coffee with the Disciplinary Committee officials that afternoon, Lin's driver and some senior officials at Shenzhen Investment were queried about Lin's whereabouts. Shenzhen Investment officials also called Lin's wife who was already in Canada with the couple's son. She said she knew nothing.

Some 24 hours later, Hu received a call from an apologetic Lin in Vancouver.

"I'm here to treat my high blood pressure. I've done nothing wrong," he insisted.

High blood pressure? That was the first I had heard of that, and my colleagues said the same thing.

"But why did you leave so suddenly? And why at this juncture? And why did you not call the Disciplinary Committee in advance to cancel the appointment?" Hu asked Lin.

Lin wasn't telling. After an hour spent trying to persuade the fugitive to return, Hu tried a more direct appeal.

"Look Minrui, I am sure you are innocent. The Disciplinary Committee may just want to have a routine catch-up meeting with you. And there is nothing I know of that they have against you. Your staying overseas for too long may just send a wrong signal to the Committee, and put us poor old souls at Shenzhen Investment in an awkward situation. Come on, fly back. Or even take a rest for a few days before flying back. Then when you get here, explain everything to the Committee. I will do whatever I can to help you." Hu had been the Secretary-General in the Shenzhen Government before and had lots of clout. Moreover, Hu was a widely respected and liked figure.

After several long conversations, Lin agreed to fly back immediately. But there was one condition:

"I want to fly to Hong Kong, not Shenzhen," he said.

Hong Kong has a separate legal jurisdiction from Mainland China, and there is no extradition agreement between the two even though Hong Kong has been part of China since the 1997 Handover.

"Okay, okay," Hu relented.

Lin also wanted all members of the management team to give him a face-to-face promise that he would not be punished for his sudden flight to Canada if he went back to Shenzhen. Hu also agreed so a meeting was set up at the company's headquarters in Kowloon for 2 the next Monday afternoon.

After that early, early Sunday morning call, I was already on my way back to Hong Kong.

I learned later on that Hu and two other senior party officials — Zhang Yijun, CEO, and Zhao Gesheng, Executive VP, both from Shenzhen Investment — had huddled up for two days in an attempt to solve this thorny problem. As is often the case, this type of personnel issue is usually only dealt with within the Communist Party apparatus.

Though I was COO, I was not part of that apparatus. In this particular case, Hu called me only because I was a member of the Board of Directors and the company's public face in the capital markets.

Lin had insisted on the phone that I be present at the Monday meeting but not because he particularly liked me. No, it was because I was something of an "outsider" and could possibly provide proof of some sort in the future if the need arose. I was, after all, one of the six executive directors of the company so I had some pull.

I had demanded in several board meetings the previous year that Lin be sacked. But I never won that argument.

I wanted Lin sacked not because I had any evidence of his financial embezzlement — I didn't know anything about that — but rather I thought he was not performing the basic duties as a business manager. Sacking a senior manager for poor performance, for being lazy, or incompetent was — and still is — very rare in a state-owned entity in China. But Lin had failed to make any progress on the real estate projects in his portfolio, despite very clear operating targets and my repeated warnings, so I thought it was time for him to go.

In one of the meetings of senior and mid-level managers in late 2006, I questioned Lin for his weak explanation as to why there had been no progress in his projects, and stated that heads had to roll if he was unable to shape up his game. In response to my urging to fire Lin in early 2007, Hu promised that he would sit down with Lin for a proper discussion (meaning a final warning). Apparently before Hu had the opportunity to do that, the Disciplinary Committee had called Lin for an entirely different reason.

The next morning, I took the earliest flight from Beijing to Hong Kong after having driven almost three hours to reach the Beijing Airport before that. You have to take the earliest flight you can get since delays are so common at China's airports. That was already a problem in 2007 and I did not want to take any chances.

That Monday was a public holiday in Hong Kong. By 2, the six executive directors of Shenzhen Investment had gathered in the conference room and they were waiting for Lin to show up. These executive directors all lived in Shenzhen, and had driven to Hong Kong on a public holiday just for this critical meeting.

I knew everyone was probably thinking up things to say to Lin to persuade him to go back to Shenzhen. I was going to suggest that Lin be totally upfront with the Disciplinary Committee, and ask for a pardon in the most sincere manner he could. I knew no senior politician in Shenzhen personally, so I had no leverage. I was sure Lin knew that.

In the end, I was counting on Hu's persuasive power.

The conference room was stuffy and hot, even in February. We waited, and waited, but Lin did not show. By about 3 or so, Hu told us all to go back to our offices to do our own things while he alone would wait in the conference room. In the meantime, he got his assistant to check the arrival information of Lin's flight from Vancouver.

At around 6, someone suggested that we call Lin's wife in Vancouver and ask if she knew what had happened to Lin. In a shock to us, Lin had not even boarded the flight, and had not even bothered to call us.

"I was not feeling well, and so couldn't fly back to Hong Kong as planned," Lin apologized on the phone.

"You tricked all of us!" Hu was furious. "How can I trust another word out of you?" he shouted into the receiver at the faraway Lin. I had worked with Hu for a year and never seen him this angry.

The six of us gathered again in that conference room before 6 to come up with a plan or a strategy but no one knew what to do. We could only agree that we had to be honest and transparent with the Disciplinary Committee about the reality of the situation.

Lin had fled not just a business deal that had gone sour but what he saw as the wrath of the Party. What the *real* reason was for Lin's sudden escape I still do not know even now.

At Shenzhen Investment, like at most state-run companies in China, after some board meetings, there would be a Party meeting. I would have to excuse myself, along with the independent directors, so that the other executive board members who were members of the Party apparatus could hold a meeting, often to rectify the board decisions. Sometimes, they would discuss other issues such as personnel or risk control, anti-money laundering efforts, or compliance. Officially, these issues would have to be approved by the Board of Directors. But Party members would have a unified position. The nomination of officials was often in the hands of the Party apparatus.

In the 1990s, Lin was a senior politician's assistant. In Chinese official parlance, that position is called a "secretary." Secretaries have power because they are the gatekeepers for their political masters. The position often serves as a stepping stone to something important in government or the business world. Large numbers of politicians, senior civil servants, and corporate managers at every level have gone through that apprenticeship. For Lin, the apprenticeship eventually landed him a job as an Executive Vice President at the listed Shenzhen Investment and its parent company (Shum Yip Group 深業集團). He also held a Board Director position. But for whatever reason, he did not have any motivation to work at all. He was also unusually quiet. Several years later, he was demoted to head a small subsidiary, Dafu Corporation, and that seemed to suit him. In a quiet corner, he could harmlessly manage only 30 to 40 people and his day-to-day job was to do almost nothing. But his compensation package and perks remained enviable: an annual salary of close to 1 million yuan, a driver and a company car, a personal assistant, and a big expense account.

In May 2007, it came time for the company's 40 or so senior and mid-level managers to gather at a resort for an offsite briefing. This time the venue was the Sheraton on Songshan Lake in Dongguan. I hated spending this kind of big money on offsite meetings like this one but it was a company tradition and I was scheduled to speak to the gathering in the afternoon.

I stood at the podium and reviewed my notes. My topic was going to be an unpleasant one. I was going to turn my attention to the "stick" part of the old "carrot and stick" equation.

During the speech, I told my colleagues that the company paid everyone well — perhaps too well — and had given everyone generous perks and stock options.

"But there are too many slackers in the ranks," I said. "Their existence has poisoned workplace morale."

We now had to use the "stick" and get things back on track and punish those who were not doing a good job.

My face turned red and I became a bit animated standing at the podium. I suggested that the company take disciplinary action against Chairman Hu and CEO Zhang, in the form of a censure. Hu and Zhang had failed to supervise Lin properly, I argued, and, despite my repeated urging, had not fired Lin. Lin's division was a dismal failure and a drag on the group's overall performance.

People in the crowd were stunned. So was I. Today, I regret the way I said what I said, but I had rehearsed my speech many times and I suspect that I would have hated myself later if I had chickened out of saying what was on my mind.

Hu and Zhang were silent and their faces turned red. I knew they were upset and shocked by my speech. They have never since said anything about my speech and somehow we have maintained our friendship since then. I knew the audience would not discuss my speech in public but I was pretty sure that they would talk about it in private. Maybe that was what I wanted more than anything else?

I fired a second salvo—maybe it was a Molotov cocktail? — at the audience during my speech. On a scale of 0 to 100, I gave each of the four major subsidiaries and leaders a score. Lin's division of Dafu was a disaster and they got a 0. Tairan was ranked the second lowest with a score of 20, despite the fact that it was the biggest profit contributor to the group. Its chairman, Ma Xiejin, was a competent and respected elder in the larger group, but he had refused to sell property as fast as I had wanted him to. That was effectively a challenge to the group strategy of increasing the group's total asset turnover ratio. I remarked about Ma's lack of cooperation with the group management. Ma was visibly shaken but only said that I was being unfair. In hindsight,

I was. Six months later in an internal meeting, I apologized to Ma for being too blunt.

The third subsidiary, Pengji Corporation, headed by Xu Ruxin, received a (barely) passing mark of 50, for the Chairman's efforts at selling off underperforming assets such as investment property (offices) and factories. They also acquired several land sites in Jiangsu Province and these helped the group to expand its footprint outside of Guangdong Province. During a break, Xu sounded unhappy about the passing grade since his team had worked hard under extremely unfavorable conditions. Pengji employed quite a few veterans from the Railways Engineering Group, a military attachment. Some of these employees were older and did not have the necessary education and training to work in a real estate development entity. Some employees used to have senior ranks in the military and might have felt unhappy about their current status. Armed with implicit lifetime employment, Xu had a difficult job of managing them. Maybe I was an ignorant loudmouth in Xu's eyes but he forgave me for being aggressive and blunt to him and other elders in the company. I had forged a solid friendship with Xu in those three years partly because of our age gap (he was 10 years my senior) and partly because we were so different. I respected him for his ability and humor. Like me, he grew up in an impoverished rural setting in central China. Our bonding had strengthened when we swapped sob-stories about eating sweet yams for lunch at school. He also praised me, a non-smoker, for being forgiving when he smoked in the meeting room.

I gave the highest score to Southside Property, headed by Wang Yongda, for their aggressive efforts to acquire land sites, and sell completed property units quickly. A year later I would regret this appraisal after I found out that this team had the lowest profit margins because of their poor control over costs. Yes, they were solid team players in my eyes, but they were also the biggest consumers of capital in the group, accounting for about half of the group's total assets and almost two-thirds of its bank loans. So, on a risk-adjusted basis, this team was the worst value-destroyer. But I was still learning the ropes when I gave out those scores and would reassess things differently now.

I proposed hiring a dynamic outsider from the private sector to lead Dafu after Lin had made his escape to Canada. But the people I nominated failed to meet the requirements laid down by the Board of Directors. There was also disagreement on compensation and reporting lines. I did not want to fight battles on too many fronts with entrenched internal powers, so I gave up. At the time, Dafu was involved in several disputes with local private businessmen headed by Ted Yin. I attended several dispute resolution meetings with Hu and Lin, but discovered that things were too complicated.

The origin of the dispute was a joint venture Dafu had had with three private businessmen for real estate development. There were claims and counterclaims of prior verbal agreements, hidden accounts, and unfair transfer payments in that era. Senior officials in the city government were also dragged in to mediate the dispute on several occasions but to no avail. I could not help but feel that some mysterious deals were blocking a resolution. This dispute consumed a lot of my time and that of Hu and Zhang. Years later, after I had left Shenzhen Investment, the result was a partial surrender by the government entity. As is often the case in China (and elsewhere too), if the private sector uses strong-arm tactics against a state entity, it is the state entity that will lose. No one is there to safeguard the interests of the taxpayers.

I suspect that the Disciplinary Committee's inquiry of Lin was probably related to that dispute.

I guess you could say that Lin won that battle as he has still not returned to Hong Kong or Shenzhen. The Committee did an investigation of him but I don't know the findings and I was not supposed to ask anyway.

2
Chapter

Rejecting a Big Acquisition: Investments Amid Fanciful Projections

PARTY MAN, COMPANY MAN

Researchers have found that most corporate mergers and acquisitions (M&A) do not produce the benefits touted by their sponsors and the investment bankers. There are many reasons for this. Through my own experience, I found that there were usually three reasons:

1. The executives involved want to grow their personal empires instead of enhance shareholder value — a common "principal-agent" problem.
2. Human inability to resist the temptation of jumping on the bandwagon of the newest and coolest.
3. The executives are under pressure to do something, or to be seen doing something. Making acquisitions seems a lot easier than squeezing value out of existing operations. When the existing operations are suffering, or have suffered for a few years — in some cases due to reasons beyond the management's control — executives are often tempted to find a quick fix by acquiring another's business, even in a completely unrelated sector. If the acquisition proves a failure, it may be years down the road. When doing acquisitions, there was a lot of wishful thinking, and investment bankers and lawyers (and auditors) often inadvertently encouraged that thinking.

In the Chinese context, and particularly among state-controlled enterprises, it has a slightly different variation, though all the above three factors are actively at work also.

I learned this on the first day at work at Shenzhen Investment, a company majority-controlled by the Shenzhen city government.

It was in mid-March 2006. I had just been hired as COO, and a designated executive director pending approval at the next shareholders' meeting in May.

Rejecting a Big Acquisition: Investments Amid Fanciful Projections

On that Saturday, I was asked to attend a meeting in Qilin Hotel, at which construction experts in the fields of toll roads and bridges, and financial experts would attend and give their assessment on a toll road Shenzhen Investment was considering purchasing. The price tag was 2.9 billion yuan (420 million U.S. dollars at the then exchange rate), roughly the same as the market capitalization of Shenzhen Investment. So, it was a big deal.

The 63-kilometer toll road, by sheer coincidence, was located in Jingzhou City, near my hometown in central Hubei Province. It connects Jingzhou City on the Yangtze River to the border town of Dongyuemiao in Hunan Province, thus it is named Jingdong Expressway.

The toll road was a "green field" project, and was supposed to start traffic flows nine months after the expert endorsement meeting in March 2006.

Construction of the road started three years earlier, cutting through a vast area of lush farmland and a large number of small lakes and ponds. The construction cost was high due in part to the soft land base, and in part to constant demand from local villagers and governments to extract extra compensation above and beyond what had been agreed upon.

The agrarian region has an income per head roughly one-quarter of the level of Shanghai. I grew up there and knew just instinctively that traffic flows would be small for a new toll road. After all, the new toll road would have to compete with a paved road that was free of charge, though the old road was narrow and not enclosed. This meant that the drivers on the old road often had to give way at intersections. For most low-income farmers and small businesses, the old road was probably good enough, and better than the high toll fees of 120 to 200 yuan going through the whole distance of 63 kilometers on Jingdong Expressway.

In the six months prior to that, a working team of six at

PARTY MAN, COMPANY MAN

Shenzhen Investment headed by Zhang Baowu (head of the investment department) did extensive due diligence on this and other toll roads, and eventually selected Jingdong.

On that Saturday, experts came from as far afield as the Ministry of Communications in Beijing, in addition to scholars, independent practitioners, the financial advisory firms representing both the seller and the buyer, the top managers of the seller (the road developer, Hubei Huayin Corporation), and the two legal firms representing both sides. It was a grand gathering of 70-odd people on a sunny Saturday morning.

It was the first time I had heard of the toll road, and of Shenzhen Investment's plan to make this "transformational" acquisition. I quietly blamed myself for having taken on a job without doing this sort of basic investigation of my new employer. After Chairman Hu and Gao Lei, a Deputy Head of the State-owned Assets Supervision and Administration Commission of the State Council (SASAC), each gave brief opening remarks about Shenzhen Investment's determination to open a new business line, and the importance of the central region in China's growth strategy, various parties started to make their cases, invariably via PowerPoint slides. These slides covered the working team's introduction of the road, their justification for the deal and their extensive due diligence, the lawyers' views, the financiers' opinions, and so on.

While I was familiar with this routine, I knew nothing about the road and its economics. So, I frantically flipped through the thick pack of documents in front of me. I was stunned by two figures: the average daily traffic volumes of 22,000 cars (which would grow in a straight-line fashion to 85,000 by the end of its 30-year concession, according to the working team and various advisory teams), and the staggering price tag of 2.9 billion yuan (including the debts in the project that we, as the buyer, had to assume).

Rejecting a Big Acquisition: Investments Amid Fanciful Projections

I was no expert on toll roads or infrastructure projects, but when I was a research analyst, I did notice the huge disappointment shown by several listed toll-road companies such as Zhejiang Expressway (0576 HK 浙江沪杭甬), Shenzhen Expressway (600548 Shanghai 深高速), Jiangsu Expressway (0177 HK 江苏宁沪高速公路), and Sichuan Expressway (601107 Shanghai 四川成渝). When these companies went public in the 1990s, they invariably made projections of rapid growth of traffic flows and cash flows, but very few projections had materialized, despite a fast-growing economy. The reason? Competing roads: both new toll roads and the government's free roads. It is said that well over two-thirds of all toll roads in the world are in China. In the early years of the toll-road boom in the 1990s, some road developers had made a killing but when latecomers started to pile in, their fortunes had started to wane, and many operators lost their shirts as more and more roads were built. The second factor behind the losses of the latecomers was the rising cost of construction (including compensations for farmers and residents who were affected). I did not know this until many years later.

There has always been tension between road users and road developers. Tolls in China have never been cheap, particularly for industrial users. Trucks attract the highest tariffs. As the costs of land and construction surged in the past two decades, so too did toll rates though they lagged behind somewhat. Transporting a truck of grain, cotton, coal, or timber from Henan Province in central China to Guangzhou in the south could cost over 200 U.S. dollars on toll fees alone. Many officials and observers blame China's high logistics costs on toll fees. In the meantime, toll road operators moan that they are making meager returns.

As road users struggle, some populist officials and politicians want the government to renege on road concessions and reduce toll rates. Some regional governments had bought roads back, or renegotiated toll rates down, and in some cases, they simply ordered operators to stop collecting tolls. In some cities, intransigent operators (normally private entrepreneurs) protested the government's backtracking and reneging of contracts, and sadly more than a few of those "tough-nuts" had ended up in prison.

Over the years, the Ministry of Communications that is in charge of the toll road sector's supervision across the country had ordered road operators to waive tolls on agricultural vehicles, military vehicles, and vehicles for environmental projects. In 2011 to 2012, they forced operators to waive all charges during long national holidays. These arbitrary decrees reduced operators' net cash flows by as much as a quarter or even a third, hurting the underlying values of these companies significantly.

At our expert meeting, when various parties were done presenting their cases, Chairman Hu asked for questions. In this type of situation, all parties would normally be too polite to ask questions, and if they had to ask a few questions, they would ask soft ones. But not me. I was the first to immediately raise my hand. Instead of asking a question, I made a statement. In fact, I dropped a bombshell. As most people at the meeting did not know me, I spent a couple of minutes introducing myself as the new COO of Shenzhen Investment, and stated that I thought the traffic projections were far too high. "I come from Jingmen, near the toll road. Based on my knowledge of the place, I reckon we would be lucky to get one-tenth of the projected traffic in the first few years. I really mean just one-tenth!" The conference room immediately became dead silent, and I saw many embarrassed red faces in the room. A few people were gasping for air.

Simmont Far East was a recognized valuation and traffic consultancy. Their staff were immediately put on the spot. Peter Yin, its managing director started to repeat what he had just said at his presentation about the methodologies of their projections. They claimed that they used data from comparable roads, visited local officials and businessmen, counted cars on the existing free road, and considered growth potential, and so on.

While Yin was talking, Chairman Hu rushed to me, and pulled me outside the room. He whispered to me, "This meeting is for independent experts to analyze and approve the acquisition. As part of the management, you are not supposed to have a view, particularly when your views are different from the working team and the advisors."

I was also shocked and did not know what to say and what to do. Maybe I had just broken protocol, and caused my employer trouble? While the whole crowd at the meeting was hearing Yin's repeated assurance that their projections were reasonable, Hu and I quickly returned to our seats under everyone's sympathetic stare. Given the significance of the road under consideration, I was not about to go along with the crowd without a convincing explanation. Annoyingly, I persisted with a few more questions on traffic flows and asked if the working team and Simmont Far East could explain why five to six toll road operators listed on the Hong Kong Stock Exchange had all disappointed their investors big time.

Based on my experience, this type of expert meeting was a mere formality, and it would be wrapped up within two hours. Meeting participants would have a pleasant lunch, drink lots of wine, toast each other's health, renew friendships, and congratulate each other for work well done.

But my stupid questions and intransigence had completely ruined the festive atmosphere. They must have all thought of me as naive and out of place. After all, all the professional firms (auditors, lawyers, advisors, and valuers) as well as the company management wanted to dissociate themselves from any legal or regulatory liabilities that might arise in the future. So, the discussion continued well after 1 in the afternoon, and the lunch was much less fun as well. After lunch, the discussions would continue. Everyone finally agreed to sign off on the expert report in the early evening, as most guests had planned to fly back to Beijing or Shanghai, or had to rush to their other appointments in Shenzhen. I felt sorry as the expert endorsement meeting had ended on a nervous note.

PARTY MAN, COMPANY MAN

The second day, the Board of Directors at Shenzhen Investment convened to approve the acquisition in light of the full endorsement of the expert report. As I was not officially a board member, I sat at the meeting but could not cast a vote. The board meeting was tense, not only because I was present, but also because the issues I raised were hard to be dismissed. As the deal had been discussed at the board level several times already, there was no reason for any board member (including the three independent directors) to suddenly change their minds. After all, they did not have any new information that would make them want to change their minds, especially since the company had spent heaps of time and money on the due diligence of the project. So, the board duly approved the acquisition of Jingdong.

But both Chairman Hu and CEO Zhang were cautious people and wanted to do the right thing. Despite the green lights by the expert report and the board meeting, they wanted to hold off on the actual purchase of the road "until Joe is truly convinced." Hu said that "Given the uncertainty of any new business, it is only fair to give dissenting voices a chance to be heard."

Clearly the burden had come to me. I did not want to stand in the way of a sensible acquisition but I did want to prevent a stupid one. I immediately started to meet analysts and people I knew to gain a bit more understanding of the toll road sector. I also got my assistants to compile a large amount of data: the cost of construction, acquisitions, traffic flows, revenues, and cash flows of all Chinese toll roads we knew. We found 33 of them. Apart from 5 toll roads in more developed cities (in coastal Zhejiang, Shanghai, Guangzhou, Hangzhou, and Shenzhen) where traffic flows were bigger than 22,000 per day, all the rest reported lower, and in most cases, substantially lower traffic flows. So my gut feelings were confirmed by hard data. And my negative stance on the Jingdong acquisition hardened as a result.

As I refused to say positive things on Jingdong, Hu continued to hold off on the deal. While it was easy to derive satisfaction from the stalemate, my working relationship with my two bosses was also hanging in the balance.

In May 2006, two months after I had joined Shenzhen Investment as COO, I also became a board member as agreed before. But that did not give me the ability to reverse the board decision on the Jingdong acquisition. After all, I only had one vote, and the other 10 members (including the independent directors) wanted a deal.

The Chairman and CEO held off on the deal until July (for four full months). In these four months, I had not only lobbied directors and the working team to drop the idea of the acquisition, but also tried to persuade them to agree to my other plans: sell non-core businesses and focus on the core businesses. The core I identified was real estate development. And the non-core I wanted to divest from included significant stakes in a power plant (Mawan), a cable TV operation, and industrial businesses. It did not take long for me to realize two things.

First, I had wasted four months and most of my "political capital" (as a result of the surge in the stock price) and had achieved nothing thus far. I had only caused tension with Chairman Hu, the CEO, and other senior managers, and created an invisible camp of "them and me." That was hardly a winning strategy, as I soon realized.

Second, I had been fighting too many battles at the same time, and alone. My strategy needed a serious rethink. I consulted Terrance Wang, who was then Chief Executive of Central China Real Estate, who advised compromise. In 1991, when I was a lecturer of banking and finance at the University of Canberra, Australia, I moonlighted as a consultant at the Bank of China in Sydney, where Wang was Deputy Head. Wang, five years my senior, was more diplomatic and had better people skills than myself.

I decided on a horse trading strategy with the "them" in my situation. In mid-July 2006, I made an appointment with Hu and

PARTY MAN, COMPANY MAN

Zhang in Shenzhen for dinner. We drank lots of wine together and I confessed to being a little too stubborn, naïve, and childish. I offered to visit the road the next day, meet with the road developer, and re-visit my position. They both seemed very happy.

3
Chapter

Horse Trading: Redefining Our Core Business

PARTY MAN, COMPANY MAN

My friends would be the first to say that I am often a pain in the neck, and not a good team player. I accept that and regret many of the things I have said and done to the people around me. At Shenzhen Investment, I caused trouble and embarrassment to my best friends and mentors, Hu and Zhang. They responded to my bad behavior with kindness, tolerance, and understanding.

On the acquisition of Jingdong Toll Road, I must say I did not handle the matter very well. I finally realized that to get anything done at Shenzhen Investment, I must mend fences and seek compromise and — who knows? — I might be totally wrong on Jingdong. For more than a decade, I had been half-right and half-wrong as a research analyst on my stock calls. Why insist on my point of view on this toll road?

So, as I promised to my two bosses, I flew to Wuhan to meet the seller of the toll road. Li Xianjin and Peng Ci, the top two guys at Huayin, the development company, received me. Li was a veteran of China's battles with Vietnam in 1979. He had won many accolades in the war, and was also severely wounded. When he came back home, he was looked after by the local government in Hubei in various ways. He was a business-savvy smooth-talker. Since leaving the army, he had done very well for himself, and when we met, he already owned a few successful businesses including hotels, and toll bridges. Peng was a good negotiator and deal-maker, who used to run an auto-maker in Fujian Province.

The pair did everything they could to make me feel more comfortable about the deal. Their presentation was sleek, and projections confident. They also emphasized that they would not make much money from the deal, as the cost of construction had skyrocketed in those three years. Driving hard bargains, and squeezing the last penny out of business partners was not in my blood, and I wanted to make sure that it was a "win-win" proposition.

Despite the pouring rain that afternoon, Li and Peng insisted on driving me two hours from Wuhan to Jingzhou to see the road. The road was well built, and near completion. I must say I was won over a bit, and maybe a fair bit. To be precise, I had probably made up my mind before I took the flight from Hong Kong. When I stood at the top of the first toll gate, looking at the road extending to the horizon on the Central China plain, I saw trees lined along both sides of the road, and lots of ponds and rice paddies on both sides, I felt enormous delight. That was the environment in which I had grown up.

At the time, China's real estate boom was just reaching its frenzy. I looked at the road, and felt that it was nothing but a giant real estate project: the eight-lane two-way road was a huge track of land, rather than a toll road. Somehow I felt dizzy. Numerous books and media stories had talked up the upcoming explosion of land prices on the back of China's urbanization and industrialization. Maybe we were striking gold without even knowing it. I was trying to convince myself of the merit of the road deal.

Of course, we all had heard the crazy story that the land value surrounding the Japanese Imperial Palace was greater than that of the whole of California before the Japanese real estate collapse in the early 1990s, and the moral the story conveyed. However, when you were actually part of the mania in China in 2005 to 2007, you just felt swept up every day, and you became powerless to retain any sanity. I was one of those powerless souls. I checked the financial history books to retain my cool and maintain my sanity. Having experienced the Internet bubbles, and having acted extremely foolishly at times during those, I told myself time and again that this property bubble would also end badly some day, just like the Japanese bubble and the Internet mania in the 1990s. "But who am I to make that type of prediction? After all, China is different. It has a vast population, and its economic transformation is truly without precedent." Or so I told myself.

I am not religious. But when I was in Australia, I was talked into attending two religious events. While I would sit there and try to find an excuse to sneak out, I could feel my body shaking amid the music and songs and the prayers. The feeling of the crowd could be infectious. I must say that you could easily be swept up if you did not have strong will power.

Here I was, near my hometown, being swept up by the real estate revival about a toll road. I was intoxicated and drunken. I was probably not entirely rational. But what the hell!

That evening, I was taken to dinner at a private club at Jingzhou City. Everyone was talking about how much money someone else had made in a land project, or private equity deal. Though investment banking was profitable, I felt lucky that I had just shifted into a better sector. In 1994, I had left a teaching job at the University of Canberra, Australia, to join Swiss Banking Corporation that later merged with UBS (another Swiss bank) in 1999.

I flew back to Shenzhen the second day, ready to do a horse trading deal with the chairman and the chief executive. I drank tea with the pair in the afternoon, and told them that I had been wrong, and, well, at least half wrong about the road. The road was not too bad after all, I told them. However, to make the acquisition worthwhile, I wanted to revise the terms significantly. First of all, the total consideration must come down from 2.9 billion to 2.7 billion Hong Kong dollars. Second, we must delay the payment of the last 200 million Hong Kong dollars until after the road performance turned out to be as good as projections in the first two years of the operations. In other words, I wanted to only recognize 2.5 billion Hong Kong dollars when we signed the agreement. Since everyone except me was confident of the experts' forecast, the seller would not be taking any risk in accepting the payment schedule I was suggesting, as they also believed that the traffic forecast was realistic.

In my mind, while the road looked very good, it was probably hard for the actual traffic to be as good as the projections. Therefore, my proposal was just my tactic to reduce the total valuation of the road by 400 million Hong Kong dollars (i.e., roughly 14%). In other words, I felt that, with a 400 million Hong Kong dollar cut to the price tag, the acquisition was probably a reasonable one.

Hu and Zhang were very happy about me having second thoughts on the road, and were willing to consider my proposal on reduced valuation and a conditional payment schedule subject to the road's performance. They also felt reasonably confident that we would be able to get the seller to accept my proposal.

The working team and I flew to Wuhan to negotiate with the seller after internal discussions for a couple of days. There was visible pain on the faces of Li and Peng when I made the demand to cut the prices. However, I suspected that my proposal was not news to the pair and that someone in my company must have leaked my proposal to them in advance. They were tough businessmen after all, and they bargained hard. Their resistance was mainly that they would lose money given the higher-than-expected construction costs. But in my mind, their profitability was none of my business and I was only interested in buying a road at a good price. The pair showed me their management accounts which I had seen at the Expert Endorsement meeting in March but I never trusted Chinese companies' management accounts. The cynical joke in the business world is that each company has three sets of accounts: one for the tax office, one for their banks, and one for their managers.

After two hours of bargaining, we were not getting anywhere. But I was not prepared to accept their original terms despite urging by my working team who had whispered to me in the corridor that there were several competing bids for the road. I did not believe the existence of a credible rival bid, as the hefty price was not attractive at all in my view. After all, it might be a nice thing if we failed to make the acquisition. I wanted to tough it out. We wrapped up the meeting without a conclusion.

PARTY MAN, COMPANY MAN

I figured that the seller, Huayin, must have become desperate, as the deal had dragged on for four months because of me, although they did not show desperation. They looked calm and relaxed. When they offered to fly to Shenzhen for negotiations with me and the working team again next week, they gave it all away: a rival bid was non-existent.

There was no new information in the meeting. Both sides repeated again and again the old arguments and supporting analysis. Eventually, Huayin gave in. We announced an agreement to the Hong Kong Stock Exchange in two days.

While cutting the acquisition price by 400 million Hong Kong dollars was quite an achievement, I immediately sensed that it was not the best we could have secured. After I got home that night, I wanted to kick myself. It was a captive deal, and we should have slashed the price much more aggressively, or just walked away.

After the announcement of the deal, while I worked hard marketing the road acquisition to fund managers, their response was disappointing as our stock price had not moved at all. As the real estate market was red hot at the time, they felt that we should focus on that sector, rather than spending so much money on a big and stodgy toll road deal. Moreover, they had been burned by other listed toll road companies and still had a bitter taste in their mouths. They were not too excited about this "economic renaissance" in central China.

History proved that my initial instinct on the road was correct. Two years after the first vehicle drove through the road, the road company was still losing money, and did not have enough cash to pay workers and maintain the road. The average daily traffic volume was not only below the consultants' projections, but over two-thirds below their projections!

Needless to say, the seller did not get the final 200 million Hong Kong dollars that had been made conditional on the traffic volume meeting projections. But still, we were a big loser in the deal, and the biggest winners were the seller and particularly the consultants. The multiple consultants, auditors, and lawyers pocketed their fees, risk-free.

As a stock analyst and later as an investment banker, I came across many instances where consultants, auditors, and lawyers served their own interests first and foremost. It is fair to say that the corporate world is full of conflicts of interests. For example, auditors almost always lean towards corporate management which determines which auditor to hire, and how much auditors are to be paid. "Independent financial advisors" primarily write opinions that please corporate management. Like auditors, their interests are aligned with corporate management, not shareholders.

There was a famous case in Hong Kong where a Chinese company was listed. In the last 15 years, the chairman (also the controlling shareholder) frequently used the listed public company to acquire his private businesses — a dubious coalmine, a problematic leasing business, and a start-up copper mine — at insanely high prices. As these deals were connected-party transactions, the listed company had to hire "independent financial advisors" to produce fairness opinions. But the chairman was always able to find friendly advisory firms to write the fairness reports he wanted. If the price-to-earnings multiple did not suit the chairman's wishes, the consultant would use the discounted cash flows method (DCF), price to sales ratio, or comparables, or whatever. They were always innovative enough to find a benchmark valuation method to suit their purpose.

After a couple of years, the acquired unit proved to be a disaster, so the chairman then got the public company to sell it back to himself for a song, again with the support of the consultants' fairness opinions. Sadly, the memory of the capital market was short, the regulatory agencies were busy, and the minority investors were not only divided but also disinterested, enabling the chairman to repeat the ugly trick again and again. If you want to pursue these consultants, you would have a tough time as their fairness opinion has a few pages of disclaimers which essentially cover themselves up in all the imaginable risks and warnings.

This is not unique to China. Before the subprime crisis in the U.S. in 2007 and 2008, major ratings agencies routinely gave collateralized debt obligations (CDO) deals AAA ratings, as they knew who were their customers and, ultimately, bosses. Many outrageous M&A deals always got full endorsement by their well-paid and supposedly sophisticated advisors — even though the layman was able to see that it did not make sense.

Until this day, I am still embarrassed by the Jingdong road deal. My only personal consolation was that my intransigence had saved the company 400 million Hong Kong dollars, though I regret I had not done more. I could have designed the payment schedule more aggressively, and I could have and should have done that. More than seven years later, the road was still a big disappointment, and I still cannot forgive myself for my horse trading with my bosses.

In the weeks after the acquisition announcement, I had sensed that the road would not be a big winner. My meetings with fund managers and industry players also made me think more clearly. I decided to push for a sale of the road. Yes. Sell it! But how do you sell such an illiquid asset? To whom?

After meetings with fund managers and stock analysts, I passed all the feedback I received to the Chairman and Chief Executive. I gave them my own honest views as well, which were similar to those coming from the capital market. I suggested two ideas:

First, we should sell the toll road to the parent company, Shum Yip, and get Shum Yip to focus on infrastructure business (toll roads and ports), while the listed Shenzhen Investment should focus on real estate development. If possible, we should lighten up on the road investment by selling as much as half to an insurance company whose hurdle rate of returns was lower than ours.

Second, I suggested that we must seriously consider selling our 34% equity stake in Mawan Power, a coal-fired power generation company. My calculation of the value of the 33% stake was close to 1 billion Hong Kong dollars. That cash should be deployed in our core business (real estate) I argued.

My working relationships with my bosses and the rest of the management team substantially improved after the announcement of the road acquisition, and they saw me as a team player after all. They agreed to look into these ideas.

Selling the Family Silver

Minus my first week at work, I had pushed for the disposal of our minority stakes in Mawan Power, but the Board refused to consider anything as they were fixated on the road deal. Now that the road deal had been done, it had become slightly easier to contemplate other things.

Several senior colleagues at Shenzhen Investment warned me that it was impossible for the Board to agree to sell the stake, as it had been a major profit contributor and its dividend payout had been one of the major cash flows we counted on. In later meetings, Hu and Zhang also made similar points.

I made several points. First, its dependable profits and dividends were a thing of the past. If coal prices were to surge, the business would suffer severely, and our stakes would become worthless. After all, the power plants' utilization hours of about 6,000 hours a year had probably peaked, and I figured that the business had little upside potential and indeed had only downside risks. When everyone liked that business, it was the time to sell it.

Second, it was a passive stake. Our fortunes were in the hands of someone else: the majority shareholder. But we did not want to be a passive holding company.

Third, it was not our core business. And if we had to have one core business with growth potential, it had to be real estate, rather than infrastructure or power generation. For a small company with a market capitalization of less than half a billion U.S. dollars at that time, it was not sensible to have more than one core business.

I argued that when looking back it was clear that Mawan Power had been significant to our profit and cash flows only because our total net profit and cash flows from other businesses were too small, and all our businesses were poorly managed. There was great potential to grow the pie if we worked harder and smarter.

I highlighted these factors on different occasions to all the directors of Shenzhen Investment. I kept emphasizing various aspects of my proposal with examples and numerical illustrations. In August and September 2006, I would write and print a one-page note on my proposal every other day, and kept pushing the same button, again and again. Annoying and tedious? Yes, but I wanted to win that battle badly. After all, I had compromised on the road deal for this disposal and other moves at the company. I had to win.

My persistence eventually won over Hu, Zhang, and other directors. After the Board approved the disposal, we discovered that there was a complex paperwork and approval procedure to go through before we could sell the stake, because our stake was held in a Cayman Island-based equal-share joint venture with Everbright International (257 HK 光大國際), another government-controlled company listed on the Hong Kong Stock Exchange. According to the original agreement of incorporation, Everbright and we had to consent to the other party's sale. Moreover, the Shenzhen government's Bureau of Industry and SASAC had to endorse the sale, so did the majority shareholder of the power plant, Huaneng Power International. Needless to say, the State Administration of Foreign Exchange (SAFE) and Department of Commerce had to approve the deal.

Finally, we had to find a buyer at a good price. Any of these steps and pre-conditions was enough to derail a disposal. So, the best strategy was to do nothing and keep the status quo. But I did not want that. I knew that some bureaucrats took pleasure in making our lives difficult but I did not want to surrender. What puzzled me most was why my predecessor at Shenzhen Investment would design the corporate structure and make it so painfully hard to unwind. Maybe it was all the lawyers' fault? The lawyers want you to rely on them every step you take in any direction.

Hands-On Attitude

Negotiation with prospective buyers of a minority stake in an unlisted company with little prospect of going public in the stock market is always tricky and difficult, but we were very fortunate to convince Huaneng Power (the majority shareholder) to buy us out at a price I was pleased with. In fact, when Huaneng agreed to our asking price, I could not contain my glee, and I wanted all my colleagues to refrain from commenting on any aspect of the deal, fearing that Huaneng's managers might change their mind at the last minute.

To ensure that the transaction process was speedy and smooth, I asked my team to avoid using the conventional document exchange mechanism within various government departments and state-owned companies. That route was too slow and sometimes important documents got lost or buried along paper trails. I did not even allow my colleagues in the administration department to handle the documents. I wanted to deliver those documents to my counterparts myself. When my counterparts were travelling, I offered to fly over to see them, waiting for them to review and sign the documents in front of me, so that I could take the documents to the next entity for review. This had avoided the problem of senior managers' lengthy travel delaying our transaction process. Some colleagues and counterparts laughed about my extreme caution, but I did not want to take chances.

Some bureaucrats often avoid making decisions on the excuse of "overseas travels." I did not want my company to be a victim of that excuse when a delicate and important transaction was involved.

My caution and the team's hard work had paid off. We managed to wrap up the transaction within two months, a very short time in the context of a Chinese state entity's cross-border unwinding of a complex investment inside China, especially given that foreign exchange control was also involved. Almost 120 million U.S. dollars in cash flew back to our small company. I was euphoric! Our stock price rose almost 15% in the two weeks after the deal was announced. More importantly to me, Hu and Zhang were just as happy that we had pulled it off.

As a result of the disposal, I had gained more support among Board members and middle-level managers who were impressed with my stubbornness. Equally significantly, they started to hear good things from fund managers and retail investors of our stock. Their own stock options also became very valuable. Senior managers were pleased to see their paper gains exceed 1 million U.S. dollars, which was not a small sum for managers at state-owned companies.

Right after this disposal, I started to work on the disposal of the toll road. Hu and Zhang started to agree with me on why it was a good idea to focus on one core business and divest ourselves of the toll road. Very soon, we formed a strategy to combine two transactions into one: selling a 55% majority stake in the road to our controlling shareholder, Shum Yip, and selling a 45% minority stake to a third party.

We gathered that it was important that Shum Yip must continue to hold a major stake in the toll road. Otherwise, a third party would not feel comfortable to invest in this new business. We quickly struck a deal with the trust division of an insurance company.

The insurer was a respected and well-managed company but this deal proved to be one of their least successful ones. My colleagues sold the deal to the insurance company in two ways. First, as an insurance group, their hurdle rate was lower than ours. Two, the transaction price we asked was the same as the price we had paid six months earlier, meaning that we were offering a discount. Kalvin Zhu, Zhang Baowu, and Niu Xudong who led the negotiations with the insurance company on the execution deserved huge credit. I sang their praises on several occasions including during a board meeting. I pushed for a big bonus at the end of 2007 for the trio in recognition of their achievement. Unfortunately, the remuneration system at a state-controlled entity did not allow for "significant disparity."

After the disposal of the toll road, my colleagues who worked on mergers and acquisitions all felt exhausted. So did I. Apart from coming up with workable ideas, the amounts of convincing, explaining, and selling were unbelievable. I do not know if I could pull them off today if I had to do it all over again.

Some friends said a few years later that I was so pumped up in my first year at Shenzhen Investment that my eyes would shine with excitement every time I talked about the company's prospects and transformations. Maybe I was influenced by the large number of stock options granted to me. Maybe I was an eager learner, fearless and clueless?

It is easy to become complacent, and arrogant. In my second year running the company, I made more mistakes, often at the expense of the shareholders. I soon discovered that I was just an enthusiastic novice corporate manager.

By March 2007, it became clear to everyone at Shenzhen Investment that the company's status as a conglomerate company had changed to a focused real estate company. The toll road business was gone just a few months after the acquisition, and the stake in Mawan Power Plant was gone. We also sold our 30% stake in a local cable TV operation, two aluminum extrusion companies, an equity stake in an electronics company, and a host of equity stakes in various companies listed on the domestic stock exchanges. Some stakes sold for as little as less than one million yuan, but that did not discourage my colleagues in the Investment Department or me. On numerous occasions, I emphasized that any money sitting idly by was a waste of resources, and that that should not be tolerated.

I also wanted to sell our auditorium in Shenzhen and offices in Hong Kong. But I discovered that the selling process would take too long, and that I should not use my political capital on these smaller deals. I decided to move on to another objective: deploying the cash productively. The year-long effort of restructuring netted our company over 500 million U.S. dollars from the disposal of 16 assets — not a mean feat for a company that had a market value of only 450 million U.S. dollars when I joined. A year of asset disposal tripled our market capitalization to over 1.5 billion U.S. dollars.

Taking advantage of the higher stock price, we sold new shares and raised another 120 million U.S. dollars in late 2007.

4
Chapter

A String of
Real Estate Mistakes

PARTY MAN, COMPANY MAN

We had a lot of success — or luck, to be more accurate — at asset disposals and strategic refocusing from 2006 to 2007. But then we started to make less desirable decisions in early 2007.

After around 2005 to 2006, the land and housing prices had started to surge across China. My colleagues at the four subsidiaries were slow to acquire land partly because they were slow to understand the boom they were in, and partly because they were less competitive and less aggressive in their biddings. China's real estate market was in its formative stage and it was still emerging from the old planned economy. There were still lots of uncertainties about the government's real estate policies so my colleagues did not want to take responsibility for making the wrong decisions. Also, to be clear, their development capabilities were severely lacking and some senior managers were probably indifferent to the opportunities before them. When other real estate companies across China were engaged in full-speed land grabs, Shenzhen Investment was lagging far behind. I was under a lot of pressure to at least match the competition. So, even while I was busy selling off assets in that era, I took several teams to visit places in search of land acquisition targets. But auction prices always overshot our internally-determined ceilings. From my own perspective, my lack of understanding and foresight also hindered our acquisitions. I must say now that I never expected the boom to be so powerful.

In early 2007, like millions of others, my senior colleagues and I got carried away by the real estate euphoria. My colleagues' inability to make land acquisitions and the general slow development pace started to frustrate me, and I developed a kind of inferiority complex. Maybe Shenzhen Investment's DNA was not good enough for competition? Or maybe the caliber of our team was inadequate? Or maybe our corporate governance was weak? Or maybe it was just that state-owned commercial entities were unable to compete after all?

I was not sure which factor was to blame. The quantity of our contract sales was tiny compared to companies that had a similar capital base such as private sector-controlled companies Hopson (754 HK 合生創展集團), Agile (3383 HK 雅居樂地產), and KWG (1813 HK 合景泰富). Some of these companies started in the real estate business later and remained poorly capitalized until just a few years earlier. But their size would double and even triple every four or five years. There were several companies that we aimed to acquire a few years earlier, but they too quickly surpassed our scale. In terms of product quality, our housing projects looked average. While I was popular among fund managers, I always declined to take them to visit our housing projects, even those in Shenzhen just one hour away from Hong Kong, the base of most of our shareholders.

I became anxious and impatient. I courted professional managers from well-regarded property developers, such as China Overseas Land and Vanke, but we did not succeed in poaching any important hires from them. At the time, property-sector professionals were in strong demand and their annual compensation surged well above 1 and even 2 million U.S. dollars. Compared to just three or four years earlier, that was a five- to ten-fold surge. Not only would our remuneration system prevent such packages, but also I myself would not have the courage to make that kind of offer to lure competitors into our fold.

In the past 10 years, state-owned commercial entities had gradually relaxed pay scales, but there were still limits. For example, the heads of the four biggest national banks listed on the domestic and Hong Kong stock exchanges had a total annual compensation of only a quarter of a million U.S. dollars, compared to tens of millions of dollars for big U.S. banks, although these banks would rank among the biggest in the world.

PARTY MAN, COMPANY MAN

The top 20 managers at Shenzhen Investment were each paid about 1 million to 2 million yuan a year — that's about 150,000 to 200,000 U.S. dollars, including fringe benefits. That sort of salary made it hard for us to attract top talents from the property sector where you could make a lot more. Our image as a sleepy state company did not help either, of course.

In early 2006, I was lured to Shenzhen Investment from UBS. I worked at the central People's Bank of China from 1986 to 1989, and then was sent by the government to the Australian National University to pursue a PhD degree in economics. Two years and a master's degree later, I labored on my PhD thesis for three more years on a part-time basis, while teaching at the University of Canberra. I soon discovered that I was not good enough for the PhD degree. In June 1994, I was lured into investment banking in Hong Kong.

Though I joined the Communist Party in 1985 while a student at the Graduate School of the People's Bank, and then a civil servant, I left the Party in mid-1989, six months after I arrived in Canberra. The Party rule is that a member will be considered to have quit if he does not attend Party activities or does not pay his dues for six months in a row.

To Shenzhen Investment, I was an outsider — not part of the Chinese state system and not entitled for any social benefits either. Hu and Zhang had made an exception to hire this "foreigner." While the base salary they gave me was the same as what I was making at UBS (380,000 U.S. dollars a year), I was attracted by the corporate challenges and the significant number of stock options (initially 24 million options, and 6 million extra options a year later).

According to Hu and Zhang, the company had made me an exceptional offer, mainly because of my background in foreign investment banks, and my reputation for being outspoken. They said that they needed someone to shake the overly peaceful and stress-free workplace. Like some fund managers they had taken note of my gutsy research reports even if, like other research analysts, I was half-right and half-wrong. When Hu and Zhang were searching for their "Mr. Fix-It," several fund managers had suggested that they approach me. They particularly liked that I had written negative research on fraudulent companies. One of the fraudulent companies, Greencool Technologies (formerly 8056 HK 格林柯爾科技), and its chairman sued me in Hong Kong High Court for defamation in 2001 and the chairman of another company, Euro-Asia Agriculture (formerly 0932 HK 歐亞農業), threatened my life at about the same time. Both chairmen were subsequently brought to justice, and were given lengthy jail sentences of over 10 years.

Since my own team was slow, and we had trouble luring high-flying professionals into our fold, I started to search for corporate partners in the real estate sector, the companies in which we could acquire significant minority stakes or — better still — controlling stakes. Amid the real estate frenzy, and a globally bullish capital market, there were very few willing sellers. Everyone was bullish and held sky-high valuations for themselves in the few cases where the real-estate developers were willing to sell. A self-proclaimed value investor, I could not accept those prices.

Acquiring a Minority Stake in a Competitor

In late 2006, I discovered an old real estate developer, East Coastland that had been listed on the Hong Kong Stock Exchange since 2000. It had been one of the first property developers in the region and it had been named "one of the top property development brands in China" for the prior five years. I knew that it was not uncommon for companies to buy their way to the top. Still, five years of accolades had to mean something. But obviously we still had to examine the fundamental aspects of the company before a deal, I thought.

On paper, the valuation of East Coastland was unbelievably cheap. Its stock price was around 30 Hong Kong cents a share but my team's calculation of its intrinsic value was three times that. The total market capitalization of East Coastland was a mere 300 to 400 million U.S. dollars. At that time, its operational scale (in terms of square footage of property developed or sold each year) placed it in the middle of the fast-growing sector, and made it bigger than Shenzhen Investment.

Ideally, I wanted my company to acquire the entity of East Coastland, or at least a controlling stake. That way we could transplant the skills and soft infrastructure of East Coastland to Shenzhen Investment. But that was not possible. Their controlling shareholders did not want to relinquish control.

What about buying a significant minority stake through their selling of new shares or a convertible bond to us? That was turned down too. Besides, they asked a sky-high price, twice as high as the then-stock price. If we were to buy a meaningful amount of its stock in the open market it would not have been practical, as that would have pushed up the stock price, defeating our purpose. After all, that type of investment would not lead to any cooperation between the two companies at an operational level.

A hedge fund, Kintadel, held an outstanding convertible bond sold by the company. Upon conversion, the stake would be equivalent to about 20% of East Coastland's enlarged capital base. After obtaining consent from East Coastland, we negotiated with Kintadel to take over its convertible bond.

As part of our investment in East Coastland, three representatives from our side became their non-executive directors, namely Hu, Zhang, and myself. The idea was to monitor East Coastland, assist them in strategy and facilitate cooperation between the two companies.

After we joined East Coastland's board, we did devote quite a lot of time to East Coastland. But I quickly discovered that cooperation was a pipe dream, as East Coastland's team seemed exhausted and were fighting fires every day. They wanted us to bid for a few land sites in Shenyang together with them, but we thought those sites were of low quality, and were far too expensive. We did not understand the logic behind their enthusiasm for those sites. We candidly told them our negative views and urged them to drop the bidding for those sites.

Chinese real estate developers are constantly hungry for additional financing, even when the cost of debts was over 12% per annum. East Coastland seemed particularly bad in that respect. In late 2007, when the U.S. subprime crisis was brewing, the global capital market peaked. It became increasingly difficult for Chinese real estate companies to raise debts. Given East Coastland's small size and poor cash flows, it was impossible to raise additional debts. But that did not stop Coastland from trying. It hired Morgan Stanley, the investment bank, to sell a 150 million U.S. dollar bond. At the time, while I had been disappointed with the operations of Coastland, I had not given up on it completely. I wanted to give it as much support as possible. After all, we had invested 100 million U.S. dollars in them in the form of equity.

Maybe I felt trapped and did not have other options. Maybe I knew I was confusing cool-headed judgment with wishful thinking. I lobbied our own board at Shenzhen Investment to subscribe for 50 million U.S. dollars, i.e., one-third of Coastland's bond as an anchor investor to support the bond deal. As this was a connected-party transaction, it had to go through some complex approval procedure. But eventually, we were given the green light to do it.

With support from the second biggest shareholder, East Coastland raised 150 million U.S. dollars via the 5-year bond, but the cost was high: 12.5% per annum.

Since 2009, over 40 Chinese real estate companies have sold more than 150 bonds in the international market. About half of them carried interest rates above 10% per annum. But the true costs are significantly higher.

The reasons?

1. The issuers must pay service fees to investment banks, lawyers, printers of documents, and other facilitators.
2. The issuers cannot use the money right away though they have to pay bond investors from day one. They need time to wire money into China. A lot of time will elapse before the money is actually used. China has maintained tight controls over cross-border funds flows.
3. Most importantly, the money raised from overseas has to be wired into China in the form of equities rather than debts, as Chinese authorities normally do not allow domestic companies to raise overseas debts. In the past two decades, only a very small number of government companies have been given an exemption from this. Major authorized issuers of foreign debts are the Ministry of Finance, major banks, and some central government entities. For the vast majority of companies (even those owned by regional governments), that means that the only way to wire money into China is by recapitalizing their China-based operating entities. That has negative consequences: the China-based entities cannot deduct interest expenses before tax. That artificially pushes up the funding costs for the company. Some corporates argue that they actually like it this way, because the fresh equity allows them to borrow more money from banks.
4. Finally, the debts raised in the overseas market, if it is to be serviced (or repaid) from domestic sources, would have other complications: only dividends from the domestic operations can be used to discharge overseas debts. That would incur additional fees and taxes (including interest withholding tax of 10%). Or the domestic entities

would have to be wound up to discharge overseas debts. Some defenders argue that this is rather unnecessary, as overseas debts will be refinanced by new overseas debts. In other words, overseas debts will become a permanent and growing phenomenon. But the risk is in the timing of refinancing debts. When you have to issue new debts to refinance old debts, the market conditions may not be exactly favorable. Indeed, you may not be able to sell debts at all in extreme conditions.

On the whole, I estimate that the true cost of overseas debts is 2 to 3 percentage points higher than the coupon rates given the already mentioned reasons. For many low-return operators, I think selling debts in the overseas market at this type of high cost destroys shareholder value, but I do not know if all managers have come to this same understanding.

For East Coastland, five years quickly passed. In late 2012, it came time to repay investors, as it became clear that the company was unable to sell a new bond to refinance the old bond. In most of those five years, Coastland's bond was selling below par, and often below 40 cents on the dollar. It was a huge source of anxiety and embarrassment for me and senior managers at both Coastland and Shenzhen Investment. Poor operating data from Coastland, quarter after quarter, had made the bond market fear for the company's very survival. Though I had left Shenzhen Investment in September 2008, I was still deeply worried about a default by Coastland. In those years, I still met with senior managers at Coastland and Shenzhen Investment often. I took the matter personally and updated myself on the situation regularly.

Luck smiled on me. Although Coastland did not have the cash to repay bondholders when the bond matured, the management at Shenzhen Investment eventually worked out a complicated asset swap that allowed Coastland to trade some property assets with Shenzhen Investment, which in turn enabled Coastland to borrow more money to repay other bondholders. This came as a huge relief to me. Right after the deal was announced, I sent a note of thanks to all the top managers at both companies, and a basket of flowers to Shenzhen Investment's office in Hong Kong. A humiliating default had been averted! I had been spared some long-term emotional anguish!

Throughout the whole relationship with Coastland, I did lots of convincing and explaining within Shenzhen Investment. My efforts consumed more of my political capital. With each quarter of weak operating data from Coastland, my fellow directors and I started to show anxiety and I started to call and meet with East Coastland's senior managers more often, and my attitude became more blunt and aggressive. The chairman of Coastland told his colleagues, only half-jokingly, that he was so scared of my aggressive questions that he had several bad nightmares about me calling him.

In 2007 and the first half of 2008, Shenzhen Investment acquired over 1 million square meters of gross floor areas in land sites. Unfortunately, some of these sites were mostly in small cities where total demand for housing, offices, and commercial property was limited. Five to six years later, the company was still unable to start construction in some places given oversupply and indigestion in those markets. This directly contributed to high leverage ratios and high finance expenses at Shenzhen Investment.

Until this day, some of those decisions on land acquisitions still haunt me.

In July 2007, amid a looming collapse of the U.S. banking system, Citigroup's then Chairman Charles O. Prince famously said that "As long as the music is playing, you've got to get up and dance." He told reporters, "We're still dancing." He might as well have been speaking for all participants in the stock market, and indeed the real estate market in the midst of euphoria. Since 2007, the Chinese government has repeatedly warned about a property bubble, and has imposed tough restrictions on property developers and even home buyers, only to see property prices escalate. In late 2013 and early 2014, while more and more people started to feel uneasy about high prices and high vacancies across the country, few property developers are retreating. Indeed, they are still buying more land, and selling, more bonds in the international market to finance their growing portfolios. Of the tens of thousands of property developers, very few are leaving the party. They are still dancing. Of the millions of home buyers who have made a fortune in the past decade from rising property prices, very few are bailing out. The prolonged bull market had conditioned us that "every dip is a buying opportunity," even when they harbor their own doubts. They may have fear, but they are over-ruled by greed.

5

Chapter

Managing People:
Motivation at an SOE

PARTY MAN, COMPANY MAN

The Chinese economy, despite a decentralization movement under Deng Xiaoping since 1978, is still dominated by the state sector. Some big sectors are almost exclusively part of the state sector such as banks, broker-dealers, trusts, railways, telecoms, oil and gas, airlines, airports, and ports.

State-owned entities still command tremendous advantages. They are often given abundant capital by the Ministry of Finance or the local government treasury, and are backed by low-cost bank loans. Their top managers often rotate with regulatory officials. That way, they keep their important contacts in the government. In the case of Shenzhen Investment, for example, Hu was Secretary-General at the city government for many years before his current position, and Zhang had been chief of the Auditor Bureau and head of the Communist Youth League in Shenzhen in the 1980s. Many of their colleagues at the time are still in the government. So, they would be able to call on those contacts for help if they had to. In a country where who you know is probably as important as what you know, this can make a huge difference in the success of your business.

Given these advantages, if the sector is on an uptrend (tail wind), the state-owned companies in the sector can make a killing if they are governed properly. For example, Hong Kong-based China Merchants Group (招商局集團), China Resources Group (華潤集團), and China Overseas Group (中國海外集團) have been exceedingly successful in the past two decades (largely due to their privilege of having government backing).

Sadly, they are probably in the minority. A vast majority of the state-owned companies either squander their advantages, or engage in destructive practices to stifle competition. They are in most cases overstaffed, inefficient, and corrupt. As a result, their returns are poor on the whole.

In 1997, Shenzhen Investment was hastily put together by the city government to go public on the Hong Kong Stock Exchange. Various divisions were totally unrelated, there were turf wars between them, and they had very little commercial synergy. In the first few years, the top management was similar to the Secretary General of the United Nations, as the heads of various divisions pretty much ran their own shows.

In many cases, the group chairman and CEO did not have real authority over divisional heads, either because divisional heads had their own political backing high up in the top echelons of the government who were more powerful than the group chairmen and CEOs, or they did not respect the group leaders (who were political appointees rather than those with good performance). After all, the divisional heads, like most of their middle and junior managers, were similar to civil servants and could not be sacked. In some cases, divisional heads did not even bother to attend executive meetings or board meetings at the group level. On several occasions, the chairmen would open board meetings by saying "Thank you very much Mr. So-and-So for attending the Group meeting in person."

Many stock analysts (including myself at the time) did not understand that, and drew the wrong conclusions on the companies' leverage ratios and operations based on consolidated accounting information. For example, we did not understand why a listed company had to raise fresh equity by selling shares when it held a massive amount of cash. The real reason in some cases is that the cash is in one particular subsidiary but other subsidiaries are cash-strapped and the group-level management is unable to move the cash from one division to another — even though these are all wholly-owned subsidiaries. So this company is a loose association, not a real business.

My observation is that most red-chip companies fell into this camp in the first 10 to 15 years (even until recently in some cases). For example, companies controlled by many city or provincial governments were UN-type clubs where top management had no real authority over divisions.

Learning about Motivating Employees

I read Peter Drucker, Jack Welch, and even Michael Porter. But my knowledge of management theory was patchy at best. Since I was usually self-confident, I felt, when I joined Shenzhen Investment in 2006, that with some common sense, I should be able to manage people, and make a contribution as I saw a lot of low-hanging fruit at the business.

But when I was at the job, I quickly discovered it was a lot more challenging than I had expected. Given the general lack of motivation at government companies in general, I strongly advocated a stock option even before I had come aboard. I asked for a lot of options as part of my compensation package and got what I had wanted.

The first batch of options was given roughly to the top 20 managers. But over time, I discovered that while options had made those who got options happy, it did not motivate them. They still waited for other people to work hard and they would take a free ride. What was worse was that options for the few had antagonized those who did not receive options. While the top 20 managers wanted to see a higher stock price so that they could make more money, no one had any added incentives to work hard. What I often heard from my fellow directors and mid-managers was "Why is our stock price not rising faster? In your recent meetings with fund managers, what was their feedback?" While I held the biggest number of stock options, I quickly began to understand that, in the long term, capital market gimmicks would only work so far and that we must create value at the operational level. Sadly, operational improvement happened to be the most difficult part of running a business.

The key reasons why we were not able to really motivate people were several. First, we had too many senior managers who do not have a clear job description. They were there because they had to be somewhere with a grand-sounding job title and a comfortable package. They did not know what to do, and therefore did not have to do anything. They were typically 9-to-5 types. But their existence frustrated younger professionals who aspired to achieve something and get paid properly. These issues are common in state-owned companies.

In the first week I was at Shenzhen Investment in March 2006, there was a management meeting in conjunction with Shum Yip, our parent company. When my administrative assistant gave me the attendance list just before the meeting, I was shocked, and could not believe my eyes. I was COO of Shenzhen Investment, the listed company, and also the main operating entity. But my name was buried close to the end of the pack. The Chinese protocol is to rank attendants based on their seniority. I was #11 in the pack. Not that I cared about the ranks, but without a high-enough rank, you would not be able to push for reforms and actions. After all, I was very curious about who the other 10 people were. Of course, there was Hu and Zhang, but the other 8 were Vice Presidents, the Communist Party representative, chief auditor, the government's finance representative, and chief of the trade union. Most of these never have to bring a single dollar of business to the company, but "important" issues have to pass through them. I took a deep breath, and began to think how I would work with this crowd. Luckily for me, I found out quickly that they were generally nice and harmless people: they either did not ask too many questions, or did not ask questions at all, at least not when I was present. I was an outsider and was known for being blunt, and they tended to be gentle and subtle. Some of them probably did not want to bother to get to know operational issues in the company. So, their presence was fine by me.

Of course, most stock options were held by these veterans and that was very discouraging and demoralizing to ambitious and hard-working frontline managers. Even for these veterans, stock options were just carrots, what was lacking was stick. After I realized we needed punishment for underperformers, I proposed reforms but my proposal was neither systematic nor practical. At every level of the hierarchy, there were people who did not have a job description. They were either retired servicemen, or party officials, or politicians' spouses or former secretaries. They could not be removed if they did not commit any wrongdoing. I felt a sense of powerlessness and helplessness.

Controlling overhead is important even when business is going well and the outlook is positive. It is not just a matter of dollars and cents. It affects morale. After analyzing the human resources situation, I came up with some preliminary views.

1. We needed a clear job description for each person, so that we could evaluate the people against the job descriptions. At Shenzhen Investment as well as in most state-owned entities, this infrastructure was lacking.
2. A substantial downsizing had to take place if we started to assign specific work to each employee.
3. We needed to learn the skills of conducting performance reviews and evaluations. In my 15 years at foreign investment banks (UBS, CLSA, and HSBC), I learned that foreign banks were not doing well at that time but at least they knew such a process was necessary. At UBS, for example, they had introduced complex metrics and 360-degree reviews a decade ago. Though many bank employees hated those systems, the banks persisted. Now I knew that despite many shortcomings of that evaluation system, it was far better than not having one at all — like us at Shenzhen Investment.
4. Based on performance evaluation we needed a way to fire underachievers and trouble-makers. But this was incredibly difficult. As mentioned in Chapter 1, I recommended firing Lin Minrui on many occasions over a one-year period, but Hu and Zhang refused to take action. Considering their reform credentials, it would have been more difficult at other state-controlled companies.

At an SOE where I served as an advisor, about 200 workers accepted voluntary redundancy packages 10 years earlier. But after they spent all their severance pay, they came asking for their jobs back — as they had not found any other gainful employment or business to do, and the cost of living (and prevailing wages) had soared since then. We initially refused to take them back — "a deal is a deal is a deal" — but their several protests in front of the city government office forced us to surrender. That was not an isolated incident, and in fact it has been repeated across China.

Just before I joined Shenzhen Investment, McKinsey was hired to perform a strategic study for Shenzhen Investment. I saw a pile of reports on my desk on the first day at work. I did not read the study as I am generally very skeptical of the practicality of the reports' recommendations although I am a big fan of the firm's research in general. Indeed, I am skeptical of any management guru. I know for a fact my senior colleagues did not read the expensive-to-produce report, either. Of course, my senior colleagues had the benefit of attending many discussions and briefings by McKinsey professionals though I did not. Some Chinese companies hire expensive consultants to perform this or that study partly for show: telling their political masters or shareholders they are doing things professionally and seriously. Maybe I am being unfairly cynical.

I started to see that the infrastructure work needed to convert Shenzhen Investment into a truly market-driven company was daunting. I began to feel quite incapable and inadequate. Maybe we could do it! But to do it, we needed a long-term commitment. My political supports, Hu and Zhang, were to retire in three years, and even they did not want to rock the boat. Did they have a long-term plan for the company? I was not sure. Their predecessors came here for a tenure of 3 to 5 years just before they retired at the compulsory retirement age of 60, and that pattern gave the employees and themselves the impression that their jobs at Shenzhen Investment were just a pre-retirement gravy train.

But Hu and Zhang seemed to be different and wanted to make a genuine contribution to the betterment of the company. That had attracted me to this firm, but from time to time the pre-retirement sentiment would pop up in their own minds when getting anything done proved frustratingly difficult, either because of bureaucratic hurdles in the Shenzhen government or employment issues. Occasionally, they would also reveal their frustration to me and a few other senior managers.

In many state-controlled companies, including the banks, telecom operators, and insurance entities, being posted to Hong Kong is a privilege and a much sought-after gig. But the predictable turnover every few years hurts the stability of operations there and undermines innovation and long-term planning. Fortunately for more such companies, things are changing for the better, as local governments have started to understand the importance of management stability.

I asked myself, "Am I here for the long haul?" This question would come back to me a few more times in those two and half years usually when a tiny operational issue required consent from the Shenzhen city government's SASAC. They micro-manage businesses like us, though we have been publicly quoted on the stock exchange and the government's stakes had fallen below 50%. Their involvement was mostly procedural but it hurt our efficiency significantly.

Humbling Realization

Did I have what it took to really make Shenzhen Investment a successful business? My honest answer was that I probably did not. I said to myself that I was just an opportunistic and selfish — though probably brave — banker. I came to the scene for the financial rewards not for the long-term success of this government company. Answering this question honestly to myself made me look down upon myself. On two occasions I contemplated quitting but did not want to give up without a good fight. I lost sleep. In those three years, I also lost a lot of hair.

Before I accepted this job, I was advised by several friends not to take the plunge into a government entity. My wife Lillian had a big argument with me. In the end, I promised her it was only a three-year assignment.

Hu and Zhang each had their own plans, and they, too, often felt powerless against the huge government machine. There were the established ways of doing things that they could not break with. Sometimes before a board meeting, Hu or Zhang would privately discuss with me a certain managerial or operational issue. We would form a common view. They would ask me to raise the issue at the board meeting, as if it was just my idea, not theirs. I was known for being direct and blunt. So it was acceptable for me to raise the issue, but not acceptable for either of them to do so. "After all, Joe is really just a foreigner, and outsider" — people would often say. At board meetings, after I raised the issue and gave justifications, Hu or Zhang would jump in to endorse it. We cooperated like this many times.

Blunt Management Style

At most Chinese state-owned entities, operating targets are not taken seriously. Many companies did not even have targets. Whatever the year-end result, executives were relatively stress-free.

I wanted to change that for Shenzhen Investment. In my first week at work, I decided to put the management's operational targets on our website, and remove a lot of empty slogans. But one week later, our website was still the same. I called Chen Fei, the IT manager, to inquire about this, and he gave me some technical reasons I did not fully understand.

I told him I did not understand his issues and I did not care. I just wanted results. He said he got the message. Another week passed, nothing had been done. I called Ma Jing, the Head of

Administration, and told her to sack Chen. One day later, the whole website had been changed.

After my Blackberry started to malfunction in May 2006, I lost some emails. I called Chen and Ma again to ask, and was given a peculiar answer: I was the only Blackberry user in the whole company and that had caused the malfunction. I called one of my former colleagues in the IT department at UBS and he did not accept that explanation. I relayed that message to Chen and Ma, and asked them to fix the problem whatever the reason.

A common problem at state-owned companies is a lack of operational verification and accountability. For example, the management team agreed to do something at a meeting. But who was going to make it happen? How much money and time would it take? If a good result was not achieved, who should take responsibility and what kind of punishment was fair?

Starting from February 2007, I introduced a rule: each of the top 20 or so senior and middle managers at operating entities must keep their mobile phones switched on, waiting for my call on Saturday. On the first Saturday, for example, someone would be able to tell me "Oh, nothing has been done on the construction site in Dongguan City in the past week because of heavy rain." I would say, "OK. But please do not give me the same excuse next Saturday." My Saturday calls quickly extended to East Coastland, our associate company, leading a top manager there to say my calls were the most stressful thing in his life.

One day, Hu invited me to lunch at Mission Hills, a golf course in Shenzhen. At the end of the lunch, he gave me a book as a present. I unwrapped it to see the title *Appreciate Your Children*. It was a Chinese language book. It is a well-known story: A mentally disabled boy later becomes a famous professor and makes some important contributions to medical research. The key reason behind all this was his father who did not give up on him.

Hu explained, "Joe, you have a lot of respect among colleagues. But you have to be sensitive about reality. A government-controlled entity is just like the kid in that book. You must not trash the company. You should take care of it, and nurture it. If we all do that, it can exceed your best expectations. If you trash it or are brutal towards it, you will get a predictable outcome. By the same token, some colleagues run faster, and some slower. That is just a fact of life. I do not approve of the cruel system in some Western companies that automatically sacks the bottom 5% or 10% of employees."

I was moved by the real story. Equally, I was very thankful that Hu had taken such steps to coach me. On Wall Street where I had spent 15 years, management coaching is generally lacking as people are too busy and too impatient. Employee turnover is high, and that encourages short-termism.

Looking back, I must say Chinese SOEs are mostly warm places for their employees and families. I was about to find out more about that.

6

Chapter

Woes of the Newly Wealthy during China's Real Estate Frenzy

PARTY MAN, COMPANY MAN

Since 2005, China's real estate prices have more than tripled, and in some hot spots such as Shanghai, Beijing, and Shenzhen, they have surged even more. In the meantime, unbelievable amounts of resources (capital, material, and human labor) have been sucked into the sector. Given the financial leverage in the sector, many companies and people have done extremely well.

The U.S. real estate boom in the 1990s might have been excessive, but on my multiple visits to California and Florida, I had never found as much construction going on, and as much vacancy visible compared to what had been happening in China.

A key reason behind all this was the explosive growth of credit, not just in recent years but also over the last three decades. In my other book, *Inside China's Shadow Banking: The Next Subprime Crisis?*, I listed these figures from the State Statistics Bureau of China:

Growth of loans and money supply, 1986–2012

	1986 (CNY 1 billion)	2000 (CNY 1 billion)	2012 (CNY 1 billion)	Cumulative rise		Compound annual growth	
				1986–2012	2000–2012	1986–2012	2000–2012
Nominal GDP	1,027.52	9,921.46	51,932.21	49.54 times	4.23 times	16.3%	14.8%
Bank loan (balance)	814.27	9,937.11	62,990.96	76.36 times	5.34 times	18.2%	16.6%
Money supply (M2)	672.09	13,835.65	97,414.88	143.94 times	6.04 times	21.1%	17.7%

Source: National Bureau of Statistics, China

I was a stock analyst in 2005, and my full attention was on maintaining my team's and my own research ranking in the external polls conducted by *Institutional Investor* and *Asiamoney* magazines. At the time, I was co-head of research at UBS Investment Bank, and I covered a wide range of mid-size and small-size stocks including Beijing Enterprises, Guangdong Investment, ENN (Xinao Gas), Yanzhou Coal, Chalco, and Tsigntao Brewery. Given my background as an economist, I also looked at the big picture (i.e., the macroeconomic issues).

However, in 2004 to 2005, I had completely missed the big picture. I did not see the real estate boom coming. I was dismissive of the property boom every time someone suggested I should buy apartments and houses in China. "The quality of Chinese construction is unreliable. If there is a dispute with tenants, how can the legal system protect me? Chinese income levels are too low for a housing boom." Or, "The government will not allow housing prices to get out of hand." For ten years, most expatriates working in China have said similar things.

In May 2005, a longtime friend of mine, Terrence Wang, urged me to take a look at the real estate sector, and I took notice. He had been CEO of a very small developer, Central China Real Estate in Henan Province since 2002. Henan has a population of around 100 million, and in 2005 the real estate sector was just slowly warming up there, and prices were still unbelievably low: you could still buy a nice, fully detached house with a gross floor area of 300 square meters for as little as 2 million yuan (or less) in the center of Zhengzhou.

In 1991, Wang was deputy head of the Bank of China's Sydney Branch, and I was his part-time research consultant while a lecturer of banking and finance at the University of Canberra.

"How should I play the real estate boom if there is indeed a boom coming?" I asked as I was still skeptical.

"Invest in Central China Real Estate. The Chairman, Hu Baosen, is the sole owner of this business and I have worked for him the past three years. He is honest and good. While still small, it is the biggest player in Henan, the most populous province in China," Wang replied.

The next day, we flew to Zhengzhou, the capital city of Henan to check things out. For the sake of an independent second opinion, I dragged along my friend, Jiang Jinzhi, founder and head of Greenwood Asset Management. We flew in, and visited two property projects Central China had built. They looked very nice, far better than the usual government housing projects I was familiar with.

We ate lunch at the company's glamorous club. In the afternoon, Chairman Hu took us to see his other development project in Luoyang, the second largest city in Henan Province. Luoyang was the capital of several Chinese dynasties, and the city has kept its elegance.

Since I knew virtually nothing about the real estate sector at the time, I must have asked some stupid questions. All property projects looked very nice to me, and both Jiang and I felt very good. Moreover, we both liked the charismatic Hu, and decided to invest new equity into his firm.

The company's revenue in the previous year (2004) was less than 100 million yuan, minuscule by today's standards in the sector and even by its own standards: in 2012, its contracted sales surpassed 8 billion yuan.

While a research analyst, I did not know how to evaluate a real estate company, though Jiang probably did. The company sent us some unaudited financial and operational data. Jiang analyzed it. But I did not. We quickly agreed to invest a combined 30 million Hong Kong dollars into the company for a 5.5% stake. To me, there was such a wide margin of safety in the deal that I did not bother with details or analysis.

Three months later, Capitaland, the biggest developer from Singapore that also had big operations in China wanted to invest in Central China Real Estate. In order not to dilute Hu's personal stake below 51% yet give Capitaland a big enough stake, Hu lobbied Jiang and me to sell our stakes to Capitaland. He offered a good premium on our investment for the three-month period. By any standards, that was a very attractive deal to us.

But human nature is unpredictable. The more someone wants

your stuff, the tighter you want to hold it. Maybe we had struck gold? We had all heard of tales about quick riches in Silicon Valley. Some of my former college classmates in China bought land sites for a song and in a year or two flipped the properties for hundreds of millions of yuan. I started to hear many such true stories. Maybe we could replicate them. So we resisted Hu's lobbying. After Hu's intense lobbying, we eventually agreed to sell the stake.

The Stock Market Amplified the Euphoria

The stock markets in China and Hong Kong were euphoric on the real estate sector. Any company with a real estate business was rewarded with high valuations. Many such companies did not even have a development team, or money or land. No matter. Their stock rallied nevertheless.

For those bona fide real estate developers, any land purchase was greeted as good news, and stock analysts quickly rewarded them with a higher "net asset value" and a higher target price, and the capital market promptly obliged.

Shenzhen Investment was a beneficiary of that frenzy. Our stock price surged nearly seven-fold from the time I joined the company to the peak in 2007. On the other hand, we were also pushed by the market (our shareholders) and our own insanity to play the game. By the end of 2007, we had amassed a land reserve of as much as 12 million square meters of gross floor area (from a mere 3 million less than two years earlier). For a company with a tiny production capability of only 300,000 square meters a year, the increased land reserves would take us as much as 30 years to complete. And we were not done yet: we were still aggressively buying land across China. We borrowed cheap money from banks in Hong Kong at an interest rate of only around 3% per annum, thanks to our status of being a government-controlled entity. But most similar companies in the private sector either could not borrow from Hong Kong banks at all, or could borrow only small amounts, or have to pay much higher interest costs.

In order to acquire more land, I travelled to quite a few cities to meet with local governments' departments of land resources or planning departments. After a while, the endless wining and dining started to wear me down, but as part of my duty, I had to soldier on. I considered myself very lucky because I was not on the frontlines of such dreadful back-scratching and gift-giving.

Among the Chinese businessmen I know, more than just a few have developed a severe addiction to alcohol and binge drinking, and given their growing wealth, they can afford to drink the most expensive alcohol every meal of every day, but their health condition is horrible, and mental conditions are not much better. I know a real estate developer in Shenzhen, Huang Ding, who has several property development projects in a big city in Jiangsu Province. Last year, the city's Communist Party Secretary, Jiang Wei, retired. He could not handle the sudden retirement. For decades, Jiang had lived the high life every day, and he had been surrounded and pampered by numerous business people. Sensing that his glorious days would have to end soon, or at least wind down, he became literally traumatized. Within weeks, he called Huang to moan. Huang bought Jiang a ticket to fly down to Shenzhen to relax. At his first dinner with Huang after he had arrived, Jiang asked for 16 types of the most expensive whiskey and mixed them up for his consumption. Needless to say, both Jiang and Huang were drunk. The next morning, when I showed up at Huang's Shenzhen office at 11 to see him for a pre-scheduled meeting, he was still heavily intoxicated, and he profusely apologized for being late by more than one hour.

In the book *Barbarians At The Gate*, there was a vivid account of RJ Reynolds' Chief Executive, Geoff Ross, doing this sort of partying with his close-knit circle of cronies every evening until the early morning. That was their way to nurture business relationships, build loyalty, and form tight-knit groups. The Chinese real estate developers do pretty much the same thing. I do not envy them, and indeed I sympathize with them. They engage in binge drinking and ridiculously big and wasteful meals every day, three times a day, and so they hardly spend time with their families or do anything else.

When your wealth grows too quickly, you tend to lose sanity. There are academic studies about many athletes, music stars, casino gamblers, and lottery winners ending up in poverty because they cannot handle the sudden change of circumstances. Chinese property developers are just as bad. Indeed, a huge number of the Chinese upper middle class suffer the same disease, although their wealth may come from a diverse range of sources. Look at their conspicuous consumption, and you can see why.

As cities quickly expanded into suburbs and even distant villages, land prices in some of these places had surged astronomically. In almost all cities, a high number of previously dirt-poor families suddenly got filthy rich, usually because factories, city governments, or property developers acquired their farmland and run-down houses. Some smart speculators also acquired such land from their neighbors only to on-sell to the hungry real estate developers or city governments for big instant profits. Tough bargains, threats, bluffs, reneging of contracts, hold-outs, lobbying, bribes, and jealousy were normal. There are enormous social implications in this land-price inflation. Many poor wealthy villagers have lost their land, but do not have the inclination or skills to do anything else. They drift on the margins of society, and engage in gambling and all sorts of conspicuous consumption. Like the permanently unemployed, these people in the so-called "Ruined Class" will remain a headache for the government and social workers for many years to come.

The Land Acquisition Binge

More than a few companies went bust in the land acquisition binge even when the real estate market was in its full bloom. Of course, when the water level recedes, more speculators were caught short. In 2008, China went through a test run of a mini version of the real estate bubble bust. For about a year, property sales were unusually sluggish, the average property price corrected 10% or so, and some developers and speculators were wiped out, and a lot of land sites were sold back to the government at the original prices or lower prices. Fortunately, right after Lehman Brothers fell in late 2008, the Chinese government staged a 4 trillion yuan economic stimulus program to prevent the country from plunging into a severe recession. That program would bail out everyone, not the least the real estate developers. Many highly-leveraged developers (such as Greentown, and R&F) had turned out to be the biggest winners.

When the boom was unfolding, and particularly after repeated warnings were proven to be false alarms, everyone started to condition themselves for a prolonged boom.

The temptation was so high that you could easily lose your head when you were in the game.

In 2006, one of the biggest real estate developers in China, Sunco China, owned by Sun Hongbin, also the controlling shareholder of Sunac (1918 HK 融創中國) went bust on the back of mounting debts and over-paying for land sites. China Metallurgy Corporation, one of the commercial entities owned by the central government, and North Star, a Beijing city government's commercial arm, had been hurt by this land indigestion problem in the past five years, also due to overpaying for land sites. The list went on and on.

Just knowing these examples and seeing the punishment does not stop you from repeating the same mistake. I should know. I would normally pinch my figures when I was at a land auction, just to remind myself that mistakes can be costly and fatal. But still my senior colleagues and I made several misguided acquisitions. These sites are either too big or small. As we cannot develop these land sites, the acquisition costs involved will be dead money for a decade or two. Some land sites are just too far away or their locations are wrong. Unfortunately, a few sites that I made subsidiaries purchase are still idle as local demand has yet to catch up with the supply. In the meantime, a huge amount of financial expenses has accrued, and will continue to accrue for many years to come.

7

Chapter

Stress and Anxiety: The Principal-Agent Problem at an SOE

PARTY MAN, COMPANY MAN

Shenzhen Investment, like most other property developers in China, piled on debts to buy more and more land. At some point senior managers had to acknowledge that it was too much. Hu was the first to ask this common-sense question: Does China really need so much housing?

In late 2007, I proposed selling a big land site on the outskirts of Shenzhen to recover some cash as well as to realize some profit. As a listed company, earning short-term profits is a constant pressure. When I was a research analyst, I criticized U.S.-listed companies for their fixation to make the quarterly numbers. When I joined Shenzhen Investment, I quickly found out that I was no saint either.

After a year-long asset disposal process, where in our portfolio could I still find a profit and easy-to-sell assets? The land site Yaobao Industrial in Meilin, Shenzhen, was my first target. It was an attractive site, right outside the old Shenzhen city proper. As the city had expanded, Meilin had become a prime location. Next to Yaobao, there are low hills covered with big eucalyptus trees on the one side and mainly bamboo trees on the other.

It was a factory site in the 1980s and 1990s, but as the cost of production rose, and Chinese currency appreciated, the factory had lost its competitiveness. The original owner of the factory had stopped production three years earlier and the plant had been left idle. Shenzhen Investment bought the site with a 60,000 square meter land area for just 550 million yuan in early 2007.

We had grand plans for the site: some offices for technology startups, two small hotels, serviced apartments, and apartment blocks. But the tricky part is that we first had to apply to the city government to have the original land use rights converted to commercial use. Some extra land premium might have to be paid to the government. To ensure fairness, the government might want the site to go through an auction or tender process.

That sounded very good. My team at Shenzhen Investment had tried everything we could to convince the government that this site was more suitable for new purposes, and that we would be happy to pay the additional land premium and bid for the land site in a competitive process. But the various departments in the city government were both bureaucratic and unsympathetic. We applied. They asked for more information. And still more information. Then delays and more delays.

We made no progress. We did not even have an indication from various government departments as to when they would make a decision. Hu and Zhang also met with top politicians to present our case, but we were nowhere nearer a resolution.

Land prices had continued to rise. I eventually had had enough fun with the bureaucrats and decided to sell the land site, just seven months after the purchase. We privately sought prospective buyers. Eventually we found a local private company, Galaxy, that was owned by the private sector that was willing to pay a significant premium (about 55%) and pay cash in full.

Some colleagues who were responsible for the land acquisition were a bit unhappy, as they had devoted good effort to the acquisition and architectural master plans. They had fallen in love with the project. But I managed to convince them to let go of the land site for the reduction of our total gearing and for the reporting of good profits for that year.

The Board of Directors convened and we quickly signed an agreement with Galaxy and announced it as such. Well, not so fast as the city government stepped in to demand that we put the land site on the Shenzhen Asset Exchange (not the stock exchange) for 21 working days so that all potential buyers in the world wherever they were could access the information and participate in the bidding. Across China, there are hundreds of asset exchanges set up by the government. These are different from the Shanghai and Shenzhen Stock Exchanges. The asset exchanges mainly handle ownership rights (e.g., a 25% stake in a business) and assets such as a building, or a factory. But their trading is not continuous. An asset may be posted on an asset exchange for 20 days before the result of bidding is determined.

But putting our Yabao landsite on an asset exchange would take more time, and the existing buyer, Galaxy, might choose not to bid. Indeed, that was a risk but the government was more interested in the process, rather than the outcome. Moreover, Galaxy could potentially sue Shenzhen Investment for damages since we had signed a binding agreement already.

Luckily, Galaxy ended up the only serious bidder after the customary 21-day listing period, and its bid price was the same as what we had agreed to in the original contract.

The funny thing in the whole process was that, according to the city government, we had not even completed the entire process for the acquisition of the land site. I told officials, "Do not worry about the acquisition formalities. Pretend we did not make the acquisition." What drove me crazy from time to time was the cool response we received from the government when we wanted to do something or undo something. Every action required an extensive and tedious procedure, until every member in the working team was tired of the deal. Luckily for me, I had left the most excruciating part of dealing with the government departments to Hu and Zhang. I was most grateful that they also had to deal with other sensitive issues such as personnel and compliance.

Selling land sites that had been acquired just five to six months earlier was indeed humbling for a real estate developer. But the market was volatile and uncertain. We were pragmatic enough and did not bother with egos.

Endless Fund-Raising

At least three land sites we acquired were either too far away from residential centers, or in areas with weak demand, to absorb overwhelming supplies from our project and adjacent sites. With big chunks of money tied up in these idle land sites, we constantly had to deal with funding shortages, despite our enviable political backing. Our slow speed at property development did not help. Under pressure, the company sold a few more sites after I resigned from the company in late 2008.

Since 2006, Shenzhen Investment also sold three batches of new shares to the stock market, and one big block of shares to its parent company. The dilution to old shareholders had been enormous. When I joined the firm in March 2006, its total number of shares was merely 2.4 billion. In the nine previous years, this figure had virtually not changed — because no one would buy its shares, and the stock always traded below its book value. But today [late 2013], the company's total number of shares stands at 5.3 billion. That's more than double the 2006 count. If the stock price had been better, it would have sold a much bigger quantity of new shares. So why the endless dilution?

First of all, most state-owned companies want to build bigger companies, even though bigger companies do not equate to higher shareholder value. Knowing this tendency, the SASAC imposed a rule some two decades ago which prevented state-affiliated companies from selling shares or assets below their book value. Although there is a scope to evade the rule, it has indeed prevented many new share issues or fire sales of state assets.

In the case of Shenzhen Investment, its stock price was often below its book value. So, from a regulatory point of view, it was impossible to sell new shares to the public. However, it captured several windows of opportunities to sell new shares. Imagine how many more new shares would have been sold if the government had not imposed the new-asset rule.

In 2003, when I was still a research analyst at UBS, I wrote a short note arguing that, had there been no restriction on the selling price of new shares, the Chinese state-owned enterprises would be willing to sell new shares at *any* price and so drive the price to an insanely low level. I further argued that they should be willing to sell new shares at two times their annual earnings, or even lower. The reason? The managers are just the agents of the principals (the taxpayers), and any new money that is raised is under their personal control. This lack of discipline is a sad and inconvenient truth for the state sector. In the report, I analyzed the private sector as well. Though controlling shareholders value their assets more dearly than the managers at the state sector, they suffer another mental illness: some controlling shareholders treat minority shareholders' assets as theirs — "My portion belongs to me, and your portion belongs to me also!" That sort of thing. They tend to run public companies they control as if they were the only owner. In that situation, they can act strangely; they may want to sell shares at *any* price as they treat new money as an addition to their wealth.

In the past decade, some state-controlled companies bypassed regulatory rules on new share issues by selling shares far above net asset value (therefore above market price) to their parent companies (i.e., the city governments), and buying assets or businesses from their parent companies at unfairly low prices. On paper, these maneuvers seemed to help minority investors at the expense of the city governments (controlling shareholders), but it shows one of these three things or a combination of them:

1. The company's management is fundamentally incapable, and the clever skirting of regulations, and the addition of funding does not suggest any improvement in management quality.
2. Micromanagement by the controlling shareholders-cum-regulators has made it impossible for the company to operate profitably and, as a result, it needs an unfair advantage to survive.
3. The sector is in a recession, or the stock market is weak.

Managing Market Values

About five years ago, the SASAC encouraged state-owned entities to manage their market capitalization. The idea was simple: heads of state-owned entities must enhance the total value of listed companies. This is a vague concept, similar to shareholder value in the West.

The downside was that there ended up being a lot of abuse by the state-owned entities. For example, in order to increase the combined total market values of their listed entities, China Petrochemical (Sinopec) may have the incentive to spin off their various business units into separately listed companies, harming their inherent business synergies. In the meantime, if Sinopec were to list various units in a grandma-mother-daughter structure, it will create an artificial holding company discount. In other words, the gimmicks will likely depress the valuation of holding companies (i.e., grandma companies and mother companies), though the combined market capitalization of all these companies will be maximized.

All these transactions are not without costs. Instead of creating real value for shareholders at the operational level, the official policy is shifting managers' attention to wasteful maneuvers in the capital markets.

Finally, the government policy is unfair as share price is determined by many known and unknown factors, and the management's effort at operational level is but one factor. Indeed, the official policy may have unintended consequences: state-controlled companies may be encouraged to sell as many new shares as possible.

Controlling Public Purchases

To fight corruption, and keep down the costs of the state sector, the Chinese government in the 1990s had phased in a series of tender systems for government purchases. In Shenzhen, the city government had made all state-controlled entities do likewise, although in many other cities, exemptions had been given to state-owned businesses in the interest of efficiency and autonomy.

Shenzhen Investment each year handed out construction contracts worth billions of yuan, so the Shenzhen government insisted that we stick with the most stringent rules. That might have avoided some conflicts of interest and corrupt behavior, but it slowed us down significantly. All construction work at our property sites must surrender to public bidding. Preparation of documents and the assessment period normally cost more than two months of time. Moreover, as costs were normally the only tangible criteria in the final selection of the subcontractor, property developers often fell victim to blackmail. It had become the industry's dirty little secret that a low-quality subcontractor would offer to construct our property project for the lowest imaginable cost, only to ask for higher prices in the middle of the construction, or else they would threaten to sabotage things or drag them on. Requirements for bidders' credentials did not help much as it was not hard for corrupt businessmen to bribe their way to the highest-grade certificates. In addition, it was not uncommon for many high-grade subcontractors to sell their credentials to lower-quality builders for a fee to allow the latter to use their brands.

At Shenzhen Investment, we had fallen victim to this type of blackmail attempt several times. As a result, negotiations and settlements had cost us much more than if we had hired the better quality, though more expensive, builders. Strangely enough, the construction industry in Hong Kong had become somewhat similar with its "bait and negotiate" system.

8

Chapter

Moonlighting:
Firing Shots at Two
Other SOEs

PARTY MAN, COMPANY MAN

In most of the three years I was at Shenzhen Investment, I also served on two other listed SOEs' boards of directors: Shenzhen International (0152 HK) and Guangzhou Investment (0123 HK) [Guangzhou Investment was renamed Yuexiu Property in 2012]. As their names would suggest, they were controlled by the city governments of Shenzhen and Guangzhou, respectively.

The main business of Shenzhen International was toll roads and some logistic facilities. I was paid very generously by its shareholders, but sadly I wish I could say I had made much of a contribution to the improvement of the operations. While at Guangzhou Investment, the property developer who was based mainly in Guangdong Province, I had been a non-executive director for about a year on a pro bono basis, and I was pleased to report that I had probably made a small contribution there.

In March 2006, right after I became Chief Operating Officer of Shenzhen Investment, its sister company, Shenzhen International, hired me as a non-executive director to add a bit of capital market knowledge to the board. Both companies were owned by the same city government, but I accepted non-executive directorship in my personal capacity and the two companies had no business relationship.

Non-executive directors (including independent directors) do not participate in the companies' operations, and usually attend four to six board meetings a year, though some companies hold board meetings more frequently. Some non-executive directors are more "nosey" and "intrusive" than the executive directors, and pay more attention to what is going on in the companies they serve, and meet the management more often outside scheduled board meetings in order to wield their influence. I confess I belonged to this group.

I found that Shenzhen International's successive top managers were competent and diligent. The governance of the company was robust and transparent. The workplace was also healthy as ordinary employees were invited to actively participate in big decisions. However, on capital allocation I wish they had been more rigorous and aggressive. For example, their principal subsidiary, Shenzhen Expressway (0548 HK) was also listed on the Hong Kong Stock Exchange. It had a low return on equity of 7% to 8% because the toll road business had suffered from regulatory changes over the past 10 years as I discussed earlier. The government has arbitrarily reduced toll rates in some cities, and forced toll road operators to waive tolls during long public holidays, and on military vehicles and vehicles related to environmental protection and agriculture.

However, this process has continued for three decades, and the management at Shenzhen International did not take enough action to reduce exposure to the sector; they were resigned to the fact that this was a toll road company and that they could not do anything else. Problems also emerged on cost controls. In 2005, instead of reducing exposure to the toll road sector where regulators were susceptible to road users' populist pressure, the company made a big investment that later turned out to be a disappointment. In 2006, the company's total asset base was only 7 billion yuan (composed of 17 toll roads spread out in Guangdong and Hubei provinces), but it committed to invest a similar sum (which later overran 10 billion yuan) in one greenfield toll road project, Qingyuan Road, knowing that there were concentrated risks and competition from a free, parallel national highway (Jingzhu Road linking Beijing with Zhuhai).

I doubt sensible private businessmen would have taken that kind of concentrated risk. It was possible that the Board (including me) had been too bullish, and had taken the working team's and outside consultants' rosy projections too seriously and did not ask enough questions. Even today (mid-2014), over three years after the road started operations, and eight years after construction started, the outlook is not getting much brighter. That has weighed and will continue to weigh on not only Shenzhen Expressway but also its parent company, Shenzhen International.

In early 2007, right after I was notified by email of a board meeting a week later at Mission Hills Golf Course in Shenzhen, I shot back an email to all directors and the secretariat that it was unacceptable for us to spend money this way while the business was not doing very well. I asked that the board meeting venue be changed to the boardroom in the offices.

In hindsight, I showed my frustration at a lack of improvement at Shenzhen International, but I did not devote the kind of full attention I showed to my full-time employer, Shenzhen Investment. When I found out on day one at work that Shenzhen Investment was about to acquire Jingdong Expressway, I did lots of research, lobbying and negotiating to improve things. If I had been nearly as attentive to Qingyuan Expressway at Shenzhen International, I might still have failed to discover any problem and would have endorsed the construction of Qingyuan. Today, the total cost of Qingyuan was about 10 billion yuan, but that was the result of a budget overfun and delays. Delays meant that it had added a lot of finance charges to the bill. One additional concern was a longer construction period that had translated into a shorter toll revenue collection period.

Doing Something Right in Guangzhou

In 2007, I was offered a board position as a non-executive director (not an independent position) at Guangzhou Investment that was renamed Yuexiu Property (0123 HK) in 2012. When I was a research analyst earlier I had analyzed this company, and knew some of their history and the issues involved. I also liked to get involved in another real estate company, to learn the ropes if nothing else. It was a pro bono position, but as a director, my legal and fiduciary responsibilities were equal to those of other directors. And I took my role very seriously.

I travelled from Hong Kong to Guangzhou many times in

that year alone just to get to understand the real estate market there. At the time, almost all of the company's operations were concentrated in Guangzhou. Guangzhou happened to be a city my employer, Shenzhen Investment, was eager to get into. But they had failed repeatedly to win land in any land auction.

I was happy to pay for my own travel. After I resigned from the company, I asked them to donate 50,000 Hong Kong dollars to my old high school, Maliang High School in Hubei Province. And they did.

Right after I joined their board, I learned that the company had committed to the city government for the acquisition and the development of two buildings opposite to each other: West Tower and East Tower. Each of which would have more than 100 floors and which would cost over 10 billion yuan to build. At the time, the company's net assest value (shareholders' funds) was just above 10 billion yuan. The West Tower was a combination of a hotel and an office complex. It had broken ground and construction was half complete. But the East Tower was about to go through a bidding process and Guangzhou Investment had obtained the controlling shareholder's (the city government) approval to bid. After the working team's studies, the board of directors also approved the plan in principle.

The reserve price for the land site sounded low and attractive — only 2,500 yuan per square meter of gross floor area — while the office space selling price was over 20,000 yuan or higher at the time.

I was alarmed by the grand plan and the huge amount of money involved. The feasibility studies by the working team must have been another bit of "reverse engineering" that meant the top guys in the company had made a decision to go ahead and then the working team went ahead to find justifications. Consultants acted accordingly. That was exactly the same as the toll road acquisition plan at Shenzhen Investment 18 months earlier.

I asked to read all the documents related to this giant project. I met with all directors individually. I also met with the working team to understand their logic. I travelled to Guangzhou and elsewhere to understand the market for offices and the hotel. Liang Ninguang, a 26-year veteran and vice chairman at the company, privately guided me on quite a lot of things. He was also cautious on the big deals, as he had experienced the 1997–1999 Asian Financial Crisis.

I was convinced that that project would most likely sink the company into illiquidity and worse, insolvency. I started to lobby for a reversal of the board resolution. True, I told everyone, the land price sounded low, but one must consider these factors:

First of all, it would take a few years to complete the construction. That meant additional risks as the market could change adversely. That also meant huge costs of financing. Second, the office market and hotel market were both dangerously saturated in Guangzhou and Guangdong Province. Why suddenly add so much supply? This project might work for a big company with tremendous holding power, but not for Guangzhou Investment that was mid-sized, bloated, slow-moving, and already heavily in debt as we were at that time.

Efficiency was another factor, I argued. If the project were to be developed by an efficient company, then it might work, as cost controls and efficiency were critical for capital-intensive property projects.

I asked each director and members of the working team, if God suddenly gave you 20 billion yuan, would you want to spend it on these two buildings, or would you do something else with the money? I knew this was a stupid perspective, but I found that it paid to think like a private owner, though Guangzhou Investment was a government-controlled public company.

I prepared a briefing paper for the Board, and copied all directors (including independent directors) and senior managers. It showed that if the company were to commit to East Tower as well as West Tower, it could sink into bankruptcy. Some directors understood bankruptcy intimately. In 1999, in the aftermath of the Asian Financial Crisis, this company had almost gone bust under crippling debts (and slow asset turns). At around the same time, its bigger sibling, Guangdong Enterprises Group, went through a high-profile, and painful, debt restructuring and caused a huge storm in Asia. Among its creditors were about 300 international banks. The provincial government had to step in to restructure its debts. The memory was not too distant.

Since then, we all agreed, Guangzhou Investment and its Hong Kong-incorporated parent company had always been heavily indebted due to their slow asset turnover and poor returns. Therefore, it did not have the means to engage in these two big projects at the same time.

To convince all involved to reverse a decision was not easy. I used the same tactics I had used at Shenzhen Investment to convince the board to sell our stakes in Mawan Power Plant. Every other day, I would write a one-page note to the executive directors and clearly spell out my objections to East Tower, since West Tower was already part of the company's heavy baggage. My notes would focus on the financial aspect one day, and operational issues on another and market risks the next.

Suddenly, things took a dramatic turn. Chairman Ou Bingchang retired in mid-2008 as originally scheduled. He was soon arrested for corruption and financial embezzlement related to construction projects. Another executive director and Executive Vice President also suffered the same fate slightly earlier. The city government appointed a new chairman (Lu Zhifeng) and a new CEO (Zhang Zhaoxing) to take over the management. I repeated all my arguments to Lu and Zhang. A few weeks later, in a board meeting, my move was adopted to drop the design work on East Tower, and not bid for the land site. I was very excited about the reversal of the board decision. Behind the scenes, Lu and Zhang must have maneuvered adroitly to convince the city government to let the company off the hook. The land site eventually went to a much bigger Hong Kong company. And until this day, the site remains a site. But the new owner has deep pockets and long holding power. Even West Tower that Guangzhou Investment had built still had a high vacancy rate three years after it started letting.

In late 2008, I was asked to go back to UBS as its deputy head of China Investment Banking. For compliance reasons, I had to resign from all my corporate directorships. I reluctantly did so, but kept in touch with Guangzhou Investment. I met Lu and Zhang on a few occasions afterwards while I was a banker, and their financial numbers spoke for themselves. The pair cleaned up the corrupt company, and took the company's business to a solid platform. Lu retired in mid-2013 after five years of impressive performance, and Zhang succeeded Lu as chairman. Both men were widely respected inside and outside the company for their straight talk, common sense, and squeaky-clean track records.

From day one, West Tower had always been a heavy burden on the developer. In 2011, to reduce the financial burden of this single project on the now-renamed, and much bigger, Yuexiu Property, the building had to be sold to its subsidiary, Yuexiu REIT (0405 HK), a real estate trust company, thanks to complex financial engineering: Yuexiu Property had to guarantee its REIT subsidiary the yields from East Tower for the first few years. The connected-party transaction, and the difficulties involved in selling the deal to investors, was done by six foreign investment banks (HSBC, Morgan Stanley, Standard Chartered, DBS, JP Morgan, and Goldman Sachs). When the deal was up for bidding in 2010 by investment banks, I was still deputy head of UBS China investment banking, and I was wearing another hat as co-head of UBS Asia Real Estate Banking Team. Despite my relationships with Yuexiu Group, and the scarcity of deals since 2010, I decided that my team should not bid for a role in this deal, as I told my colleagues at UBS that "it would be extremely hard to sell the deal to public investors." I was proven wrong on this, as the six banks eventually did the "mission impossible" after over a year working on it, bashing various financial engineering scenarios against each other.

In early 2008, while I was focusing on the bad idea of East Tower, I looked at the other blunder of the company. The company had more than 600,000 square meters of investment property, but the net returns from this portfolio were merely 100 million yuan or so per year despite face value of more than 10 billion yuan. Either these property units were grossly overvalued (overstated), or poorly managed. The truth was a combination of the two factors.

At my requests, several meetings were held to discuss ways to unlock value in the portfolio: should we sell some units, which units should go first, and how to go about it?

After Lu and Zhang came to run the business, the whole portfolio was substantially reduced to free up capital for land acquisitions and property development. Sadly, I left the board directorship before I could see any tangible results.

9

Chapter

The Party is Everywhere

In 1985, I became a member of the Communist Party while at the Graduate School of the People's Bank of China. While that membership was not essential, it was important for me to get a sought-after job at the head office of the People's Bank of China, and later secure the privilege to study in Australia on government scholarships.

After I left China for Australia in January 1989, I dropped that membership automatically. In 1994, I came to work in Hong Kong and never had any contact with the Party.

Today, the Party boasts a membership of 80 million and it is still not a club that you can join at will. For some people, it takes many years of effort just as it took me. In every government entity, every level of government, and even in most private-sector entities, there are Party organizations. They are separate from the executive structure but above the executive structure. I was no stranger to that dual governance system.

In the vast majority of organizations, the Party structure and the executive structure overlap significantly or even completely. Therefore, separate meetings are just a formality. The head of an organization is often the head of the Party apparatus, but there are exceptions.

Social Objectives and National Service

In government-controlled companies, the allegiance of the managers is to the Party. That allegiance is sometimes at odds with the shareholders' efforts to maximize profits. This is especially true when the government has only a minority stake.

The conflict is often reflected in strategic directions of the company. For example, the telecom companies' spectrum applications and their choice of mobile standards, the airlines' major capital expenditure programs, the oil companies' acquisitions (or mergers), the banks' geographical expansions, and mining companies' strategic alliances are often determined by the Party.

On the personnel appointments of all government-affiliated companies, it is clear that the Party is pulling all the strings and that other shareholders have virtually no say. Watch the musical chair movement at the five biggest banks, and the three telecom operators. Look also at the personnel changes at the three oil and petrochemical companies. These movements are entirely the designs of the Party.

In 2010, the Global Universities Sports Meet was held in Shenzhen. To improve the local infrastructure (including roads, light poles, town halls, and hotels), the governments in Shenzhen and Guangdong simply issued decrees on how much each company had to contribute, and what type of work each company had to undertake at their own expenses. When a city government's local tax revenue was short for a particular year, it simply told several companies to pay the taxes for the next year or even two. This happened to state-controlled companies more often, but private-sector companies were not immune from the abuses.

Semi-Government Services?

In the 1980s and 1990s, Chinese government-controlled companies incorporated overseas were called red-chips or window companies. Their mission was to raise money overseas and bring it into China. Shenzhen Investment, Shanghai Industrial, Beijing Enterprises, Guangzhou Investment, and China Resources were all such examples. They were also the concierge services providers and tour guides for various host governments.

In the 1990s, Shenzhen Investment even provided visa services for foreign visitors to Shenzhen and Guangdong. It also performed some of the supervisory functions for other companies affiliated with the Shenzhen government that were operating in Hong Kong.

After I joined Shenzhen Investment in March 2006, I found out that the company had around 10 chauffeured cars that had permits to cross the Hong Kong-Shenzhen borders at any time and that these cars were very busy. I also learned that each of these permits cost up to 1 million yuan. They were also hugely expensive to maintain. Shenzhen officials, their relatives, and friendly parties routinely used the services of these cars. The line between government duties and personal use was blurred. It was not clear if the cars and drivers' work had anything to do with Shenzhen Investment.

A capitalist at heart, I did not like this sort of ambiguity. I decided to clamp down on this type of abuse of shareholders' money. I had a little credibility on this front as I had turned down the company's offer of a chauffeured car as part of my fringe benefits package when I joined. I took public transportation to work in Hong Kong. Sometimes I finished meetings in Shenzhen at 9 at night and I would then take a train back to Hong Kong and get home at 11.

I chose the May 2007 Golden Week as the time to make my first statement. Some years earlier, the central government decided to lump a few weekends together to create a Golden Week holiday each year with the intention of stimulating consumption. In the 2007 Golden Week, our chauffeured cars were busier than ever: Shenzhen officials, their relatives, and friends came to Hong Kong to do shopping. I told our administrative managers to hand over the record of car users for the week, so that I could determine whether these cross-border trips were really relevant to our business. Predictably, of course they were not!

I asked Hu and Zhang what we should do to plug the loophole on May 5 when we returned to work. The pair kept quiet, and did not want to say anything. When I urged them to meet to talk about this matter again the second day, they said that they had their hands tied on this front, as the chauffeured cars were a tradition at the company, and were common among other "window" companies, listed or otherwise, based in Hong

Kong or other parts of China. In addition to these chauffeured cars with double license plates, the company had maintained many other vehicles. Although the scale of our business was small, our administrative expenses ran up to 400 million Hong Kong dollars (50 million U.S. dollars) a year in 2007. The figure was much bigger than private-sector companies with five or six times our sales such as Agile Property and Hopson. I wanted Hu and Zhang to appreciate the scale of our corruption. They told me that if we suddenly refused chauffeured car services for "our old friends" and political masters, they could potentially make life difficult for us, and it was probably wise for us to keep the status quo. They also argued that the car service was probably a cheap way to enhance our shareholders' interests.

I did not accept that argument, and did not want to maintain the status quo. I also knew I was too small to make a difference to Shenzhen Investment, let alone elsewhere in the state sector. "But if everyone thinks that way, the state sector will be doomed. Who is there to speak for shareholders?"

Predictably, none of the 30-odd groups of people who used our chauffeured cars were able to give me a reason why they came to Hong Kong. All these trips were signed off on by either Hu or Zhang or another director. I raised this cost issue again in several board meetings. My fellow directors shrugged and did not come up with a suggestion. Eventually, I suggested that we move the cost base to our parent company, Shum Yip.

If I wanted to do battles, I could find targets every day. In the summer of 2007, I forced the company to change the venue of a two-day management offsite meeting from Sheraton Hotel in East OCT Town to the office. Although more than 60 non-refundable guest rooms and conference rooms had been booked and paid for, I insisted on not wasting the money, and making a statement. A few weeks earlier, when the venue had been booked, I was not aware of this company tradition of splurging for a grand hotel for company offsite meetings.

PARTY MAN, COMPANY MAN

Reluctantly, my fellow directors agreed to my demand. The meeting was held in our own auditorium, which was rarely used. It was dusty and a bit strange for the 60-odd employees to meet in a big auditorium, but I made a point. Later on, I suggested to Hu and Zhang that we should sell the auditorium since we rarely used it.

In June, an executive director of both Shenzhen Investment and Shum Yip led a team of managers who had dual roles at our parent company and Shenzhen Investment to visit Saipan Islands where Shum Yip had some near-bankrupt textile factory. It came to my attention that several members had their expenses reimbursed at the listed company. That was probably nothing unusual before, but I was very unhappy about it. To make a point, I asked the accounts department to reverse the reimbursement, and make a clear distinction between the two entities in the future.

Most top managers at Shenzhen Investment had dual roles at Shum Yip. But they were paid by the listed company. That created several problems in my view. First, there was inevitably a conflict of interest from time to time.

Second, their expenses were borne mostly by the listed company and that was unfair.

Finally, the listed company did not have a full-time chairman, or CEO. The opportunity cost was far bigger than their compensation, I argued on many occasions. But these arguments fell on deaf ears. I did not succeed in having this policy changed. I knew I was unable to that, as these decisions are in the hands of the higher levels of the Party apparatus.

To show my displeasure at these senior managers taking the listed company's time to perform Shum Yip's duties, I asked the Accounts Department to deduct their wages for the three days they were absent from the listed company. That proposal, too, did not get anywhere.

Hu was 14 years my senior, and Zhang 10 years my senior. They had always been patient with me, and so they gave me a high level of autonomy. They must have taken a lot of heat from various parties for my blunt style of doing things. I was very grateful for both of them.

In the summer of 2007, Meizhou, a poorer region of Guangdong Province, suffered a "100-year flood." Zhang grew up there and had strong emotional ties there. He organized a charity program in Shenzhen. To show my gratitude to him, I donated 200,000 yuan to his charity efforts. At the same time, his Shenzhen-based friend, well-known heart surgeon Li Jianlin, who had volunteered to work for a year in a hospital in Xinjiang Uyghur Autonomous Region, was raising money to buy a set of X-ray equipment for his hospital, and I donated 100,000 yuan.

Hu and I came from the same region of Jingzhou (Jingmen City used to be part of Jingzhou), Hubei Province. In 2010, over two years after I had left Shenzhen Investment, I donated 400,000 yuan from the sale of my books to build a playground at Maliang School, where I graduated. I had asked Hu for permission to have the playground named after him as my way of showing gratitude. But he firmly turned it down. The place was eventually named with my name against my wishes. But I must confess that I still feel good about it.

After I donated the money to Maliang School, the playground was built within two months. Judging from the photos the school sent to me, things were great. The town government wanted to have a little celebration at the opening, and invited me to attend and speak. But I was tied up in frantic deal-chasing at UBS Investment Bank during those few weeks, so they asked my parents or my sister to attend on my behalf. Eventually, Yuqing, my 60-year-old sister, attended and spoke briefly at the ceremony. Yuqing and her husband are peasant farmers and live less than 500 meters away from the school, and she sells red bean cakes in the town for a living while her husband ploughs farmland with a tractor for fellow villagers. Together with her husband, they probably make 3,000 yuan a month on average. Money was always tight, but they own their house in Maliang (a gift from me in recognition for her taking care of me when I was little), and they make ends meet. When I committed to donate 600,000 yuan to the school, with a first instalment of 400,000 yuan, my parents hesitantly asked me if I should give the money as gifts to my sister instead. They could use the money to live better in their retirement. I was a selfish soul and I loved my sister, but this donation to the school was part of my dream, I explained to my parents. Everyone understood it, and was happy the project went smoothly. The local newspaper *Jingmen Daily* carried a story with photos about "Joe Zhang Playground," and the old boys who went to school with me there 35 years ago were talking about it. I feel good about it. I would have felt better if the playground was named the "Hu Aimin Playground," but Hu would not allow it.

10
Chapter

Falling into the Arms of the State: M&As at an SOE

PARTY MAN, COMPANY MAN

In China, the state sector is everywhere. They not only monopolize (or nearly monopolize) many "strategically important" sectors and industries (defense, tobacco, ports, airports, transportation, education, oil and gas exploration, power generation, hospitals, etc.), but they also maintain massive operations in mundane and competitive sectors such as manufacturing, metals, food and beverages, gas and water utilities, retail operations, hotels, and real estate.

In many cases, state-owned enterprises (SOEs) take advantage of their status to gobble up private-sector operators, taking advantage of the latter's weakness. SOEs' advantages are clear and significant.

> **//The state has full control of lucrative and important sectors, from the banks, insurance, to utilities, infrastructure, oil, gas, telecommuications, and tobacco. //**

First, they are always politically correct, as being a state-sector operator is still the gold standard of China business. They can do no wrong. Even if they are in the wrong (for example, defrauding customers, evading taxes, or violating license conditions), they are easily forgiven while private-sector rivals (once found to be offenders) may face severe penalties such as the arrest of their owners and managers, fines, suspension of business licenses and even financial ruin.

Second, believe it or not, SOEs are generally better organized than their private-sector rivals. Most Communist Party members might not have attended Harvard Business School MBA courses, but the Party has had seven decades to fine-tune its organizational and governance skills. They can teach private entrepreneurs a thing or two about managing companies. In comparison, the private-sector has had a history of only three decades (after a long period of Communist cleansing between 1949 and the early 1980s). Importantly, in the first two of the three decades, the private sector still had a questionable legitimacy. Even today, most entrepreneurs feel that they live in the long shadows of the state sector. A large number of them feel insecure about even their lives and families. They hedge their bets, politically and financially. They do not want to, or cannot afford to, have too long-term a commitment. There is the need, the urge, the thrill, and therefore the habit, to hide things from the government and the public. One-man bands are common. Three-sets of accounts are not uncommon: one set for the taxmen, one for the banks, and one for themselves. Some jokingly say there is another set of accounts just for their wives. In comparison, most SOEs are not one-man shows, and there are checks and balances installed from day one. Their governance is more stable and transparent. Their financial accounts are also clearer and more dependable.

Third, SOEs have more reliable access to finance, and their cost of funding is also much lower. When there is turbulence (as there is all the time — sometimes due to the natural volatility of the market, sometimes due to changes of regulations or of the political environment), private-sector operators can be brought to their knees, and become the meat of SOEs. There are many happy public-private-partnerships, but there are also a lot of shotgun marriages.

> **In terms of corporate governance, the private sector has proven weaker than the state sector thus far. It is a sad reality.**

Finally, because of their political status, SOEs generally find it easier to obtain government concessions as the local governments feel more secure dealing with government-controlled entities although the latter may be controlled by local governments of another city. In awarding a contract to an SOE, local politicians and bureaucrats do not have to worry about the suspicion that they may have taken bribes from business partners, or may have given favors to friends and relatives. This type of self-censorship plays a big role in the SOEs' winning of government contracts at the expense of their private sector rivals. As the government is still by far the biggest customer in China, self-censorship on the part of politicians and bureaucrats has created an unfavorable environment for the private sector.

For example, SOEs are far more likely to win concessions in gas utilities, water treatment, infrastructure construction (ports, roads, airports, city halls), and mining. Many private sector entrepreneurs moan about the unfairness, but there is little they can do to change the bias. Imagine you are the mayor of a mid-size city. Now you have to hand out a gas utilities concession. No matter how sleek the presentation or tender documents of private sector bidders may be, you face a huge conundrum. The SOE bidders may not have a better track record, and may not be better qualified, and their offers may not be more attractive. But you know the reality: your political enemies may later on question your motive in granting a concession to a private-sector operator. So you cover yourself by having many expert committees and advisors. But these maneuvers may not be enough to help you when you need help the most, like a few years later when your political enemy may stab you in the back. After all, you never know if the private-sector operators have committed wrongdoings elsewhere or not. Even that can bounce to your city to hurt you. The private sector companies' financing may be stretched as they operate in multiple cities and across multiple business lines and you just do not know. If the controlling shareholders or the senior managers of the private sector operators get arrested for a totally unrelated matter (such as a violation of traffic rules, or domestic violence), or weighed down by a protracted divorce case, your city's gas utilities operation will be adversely affected. You do not want that extra trouble.

So what do you do? You play it safe. You award the contract to an SOE and there are lots of them around. After all, many SOEs provide better terms in their offers because their funding costs are considerably lower, and their tolerance for risks is higher and hurdle rate of returns is lower.

I have seen this myself, time and again. In September 2008,

after I resigned my role as Chief Operating Officer from Shenzhen Investment, I returned to work for UBS. This time, I switched from a research role to a banking job. As deputy head of China investment banking, I helped corporate clients raise money in the form of new equity and bonds. I served a wide range of clients, particularly in the sectors of real estate, consumer products, and utilities. I have seen how city governments awarded contracts.

A Marriage Made in Heaven?

When I was a stock analyst, I followed gas utilities companies such as China Gas (0384 HK中國燃氣), ENN (2688 HK新奧能源), and Beijing Enterprises (0392 HK北京控股). So after I returned to work for UBS, I naturally became the Principal Coverage Banker of the three companies for UBS. That is to say that I represented UBS in order to maintain relationships with them and offer them services. I have seen how they grew and their tales are very revealing to the complex relationships between the state sector and private sector.

Fast-growing ENN, based in Langfang, a one-hour drive from Beijing, is a pure private sector company, providing gas utilities in almost 100 Chinese cities. Until 2010, China Gas had done pretty much the same except that an obscure government entity under the State Council's Taiwan Affairs Office owned a stake of it and had held two seats on the Board of Directors (including the chairmanship). Its footprint was big and wide, as its operations span over 100 cities. Initially, the government stake was almost 20%, though it had been selling down in the open market to 2% to 3% in the lead-up to 2010. Sinopec, the central government-owned chemical company, owned another 5% passive stake.

On December 17, 2010, China Gas's Chief Executive Officer and a significant shareholder (holding roughly 9% of total shares), Liu Minghui, was detained by the police in China on "corruption" allegations. According to the company's announcement and media reports, there was a dispute between the Chairman and Liu, but the exact nature of the dispute has not been made clear to the public even until now. The pair has been engaged in battles in the legal and public domains since then.

Everyone knew the strategic significance of the gas utilities business. It was clear that the future of China Gas was hanging in the balance and that the uncertainty was not good for the safe operations of sensitive gas utilities in many cities. China Gas also happened to be an extremely leveraged entity, and there were concerns that banks might start to pull loans from it.

China Gas employed over 20,000 people in over 100 cities. Its shareholder structure was diverse, including Korea's SK Group, the Asian Development Bank, Oman Oil, India's Gail Corporation, Sinopec, Liu, and the State Council's Taiwan Affairs Office.

So, I saw a win-win deal between China Gas and ENN. As ENN was stable, well-run, reputable, and bigger in terms of stock market values, I proposed that ENN should take over China Gas with the assistance of some new share sales, a bond, and bank funding. After Wang Yusuo, the chairman and the controlling shareholder of ENN heard my proposal, he immediately shook his head, "No, no, no. We are just a humble private sector operator. It is not a good idea to do daring things. Why should we suddenly become that big? It is risky to be too big. You know that." As if to convince himself, he repeated these lines several times.

I was disappointed, but did not give up. I searched for another angle to convince ENN to pull the trigger. But on the second day, I got a call from ENN's Group CEO, Yang Yu: Chairman Wang had second thoughts and my idea was indeed attractive after all. There was a new twist: ENN wanted to form a consortium with CNOOC (China National Offshore Oil Corporation), which was controlled by the central government, to do the deal, instead of going it alone. ENN would take the lead role in the consortium. This way, ENN could minimize both political and financial risks.

People with business experience in China should understand the clever design of this deal structure. Chairman Wang had spoken with Chairman Fu Chengyu at CNOOC, and the two chiefs had agreed in principle to work together on this deal. The consortium had also appointed UBS as its sole advisor.

Excited, I mobilized my colleagues to work on a detailed proposal and calculations. We had also arranged meetings with lawyers, and the working teams of ENN and CNOOC.

As ENN, China Gas, and CNOOC were all public companies listed on the Hong Kong Stock Exchange, there were regulatory issues on the Hong Kong side as well as the China side, apart from operational and financial issues.

Several months passed, the deal was not going as smoothly as expected. The central government had moved Chairman Fu from CNOOC to head Sinopec which was already a 5% shareholder of China Gas. We did not know if the new management at CNOOC would be equally interested in the deal. In any case, the new chairman of CNOOC wanted more time to understand the issues involved and this deal was just one of many items on his full plate. We were also eager to ascertain if Chairman Fu would commit Sinopec to the deal. Fu also needed more time to get to know his new company. In the meantime, China Gas had gone through an eventful period: The chairman was sacked. An independent director was made Chairman. The former CFO (Eric Leung) and another executive director (Pang Yingxue) were made co-managing directors. They immediately started frantically visiting and receiving bankers to assure them that the company's operations were safe and sound. The new management also had to reassure over 100 host city governments, employees, suppliers, and customers that the ship was steady despite the turbulence.

The biggest hurdle to our deal was that Liu and one other major shareholder had resisted a sell-out, and soon we learned that CNOOC did not seem too keen on a complex deal. Finally, Sinopec had been non-committal as it needed more time to consider the implications. In June 2011, I left UBS to become Chairman of Wansui Micro Credit Company in Guangzhou, leaving my colleagues to continue to labor on.

A Predator?

After some months of behind-the-scenes negotiations, ENN and Sinopec eventually launched an uninvited bid for China Gas, but this time with Citigroup as the consortium's advisor.

In early 2012, the shares of China Gas resumed trading after several weeks of suspension. Liu's friends and partners at Fortune Oil started to increase their holdings of China Gas via open market purchases. As the stock's price surged, ENN saw a limited margin of safety and lost its appetite for the deal. In late 2012, Liu was released by the police without a charge, and he subsequently regained his board seat, and CEO position. ENN and Sinopec dropped their joint bid for control. It all seemed certain that China Gas had gone back to where it had started.

Not that simple. In early 2013 Beijing Enterprises Group made a surprise announcement that it had accumulated almost a 20% stake in China Gas through off-the-market purchases. It had become the single biggest shareholder. In late 2013, two representatives of Beijing Enterprises Group became board members of China Gas, and one of them was made Chairman. Although the board structure and shareholding remain diverse, it is too early to say that Beijing Enterprises Group is now firmly in control of China Gas. However, I feel that with the rising stock price and the sell-down of shares by satisfied early shareholders, Beijing Enterprises Group would gain firmer control of China Gas.

Indeed, in November 2013, Beijing Enterprises announced the selling of some gas utilities projects to China Gas, and that would translate into higher stakes in the latter. With more of this type of transaction, China Gas will effectively become part of Beijing Enterprises Group.

Beijing Enterprises operates gas utilities in Beijing, the largest gas utilities project in the country. It has a market value of 11 billion U.S. dollars, and strong financial and political backing from the city government of Beijing. More importantly, it has enjoyed a taste of success in the past six to seven years under two consecutive management teams.

The Sweet Taste of Success

Beijing Enterprises went public in 1997 as a "red-chip window company." Red-chips are Chinese-controlled companies incorporated overseas but with major operations inside China. Window companies were government-controlled companies with the original mission of attracting foreign capital into China. The three SOEs I served as a director of all fall into this category.

Like my former employer, Shenzhen Investment, Beijing Enterprises was just an assortment of businesses with no synergistic potential and no growth prospects: Yanjing Brewery, Sanyuan Dairy, Great Wall Ticketing Office, a toll road, and a water supply factory. The then-management had no prior experience in business, and were mostly senior bureaucrats near retirement. But in 2004, the two senior bureaucrats (Yi Xiqun and Zhang Honghai) who took over the place were different. Like my two bosses at Shenzhen Investment, Yi and Zhang were ambitious and honorable people. Although they were career bureaucrats and had no prior business experience, they were eager to learn and were fast learners. They often invited bankers, analysts, lawyers, and entrepreneurs to give them lectures.

Despite political constraints, the pair had led a competent team to acquire Beijing Gas from the city government, improve the performance of Yanjing Brewery, sell off weak units, and acquire promising businesses. The skills they exhibited in the takeover of China Gas came from their training in the acquisition and subsequent improvement of Zhongkecheng Water after 2008.

PARTY MAN, COMPANY MAN

Zhongkecheng was a small wastewater treatment company set up by a group of businessmen headed by Hu Xiaoyong and Zhou Min around 1998. Through clever negotiations and diligent management, they grew the business to four treatment plants. In 2005, they managed to pull off a big deal: acquiring the underfunded and withering research center in Chengdu of the former Ministry of Nuclear Industry. That deal gave Zhongkecheng some good scientists and credibility. Equally, it gave them the bragging rights in their subsequent marketing for deals.

Beijing Enterprises had already been in the fresh water supply and wastewater treatment business, but it had never had the scale or an aggressive management team. In other words, this line of business had been another "me-too" project.

Having successfully acquired Beijing Gas Corporation and improved its performance significantly, the top brass at Beijing Enterprises had decided to shake up the water business unit. They liked the management team at Zhongkecheng and saw great potential in them. Yi and Zhang muscled all their persuasive power and capital-market skills, and talked Zhongkecheng's owners into selling the whole business to a listed shell company which Beijing Enterprises had taken control of in the stock exchange of Hong Kong for newly-issued shares. In other words, this deal was largely a share-swap, in which Beijing Enterprises had retained majority control of the enlarged water business. Subsequent to the acquisition, Beijing Enterprises invested more money into Beijing Enterprises Water to support its rapid growth.

At the time of the deal in 2008, the listed water business had a market capitalization of less than 300 million U.S. dollars. Today, it boasts a market capitalization of 5 billion U.S. dollars. Its rise looks unstoppable amid new deals across China, Malaysia, and Europe.

What made it such a success? I think it was a combination of several factors.

First, there was the infusion of capital (abundant and much cheaper capital) and political legitimacy into a capable and motivated team. The internal rate of returns in China's wastewater treatment industry is around 8%. Given the prime lending rate of around 6% in the Chinese domestic market, and higher funding costs for a small business like Zhongkecheng, the economics had been relatively weak. As a small business, Zhongkecheng could not even dream of tapping the overseas capital market. So the team's winning formula had been their efforts to push up the internal rate of return to closer to 10% or even more, far above the industry average. Now as part of Beijing Enterprises Group, their cost of funding had fallen sharply to 3% to 4% from overseas capital markets. The appreciation of the yuan against the U.S. dollar also helped the "carry trade."

Second, the management team at Zhongkecheng reported a much more equal status since they changed their corporate name to Beijing Enterprises Water. Before they became part of Beijing Enterprises Group, Zhongkecheng begged local governments for concessions and opportunities. But after the transition in 2008, they were on an equal footing with city governments so they could negotiate with city governments for better terms.

In a relationship-driven environment like China, having the right parentage is critically important. In the team's marketing or operations, the toughest negotiations are often left to Yi and Zhang, whose visits or calls often mean the make or break of a deal or vastly different terms and conditions. The counterparties, knowing the political and financial backing of the team, are now far more willing to agree to do business or compromise on terms and conditions of deals.

Several wastewater treatment companies in China have suffered major losses as a result of disputes with their host city governments. These disputes often involve the calculation of rates of returns, maintenance of water plants, and the schedule of payments the local governments had agreed to with operators.

Commercial contracts are never watertight, and are subject to interpretations: There are always unexpected issues (unknown unknowns) that have not been defined in the contracts. When new politicians take charge of your host city government, there are risks of another round of reviews of contracts. But the team at Beijing Enterprises Water has peace of mind, as they know they are on equal terms with their local host governments.

Far from Isolated Cases

The success of Beijing Enterprises Group in making acquisitions by taking advantage of private-sector rivals' weakness was far from an isolated incident. Many other SOEs have taken a similar strategy. The only thing SOEs have to do is "wait and strike," to borrow the language of an analyst based in Beijing. He argues that opportunities abound as the economy is volatile, policy changes are unpredictable, and a big number of private entrepreneurs are aggressive and, therefore, vulnerable.

The list of SOEs acquiring private sector rivals is long and growing. Some of the recent such cases include:

1. Shanghai Industrial's (0363 HK 上海實業控股) takeover of New China Land (0563 HK 上實城市開發). The latter was overly leveraged and its former chairman had issues with the Hong Kong regulators.
2. SOE Greenland taking over SPG Land (0337 HK 綠地香港). The reason? The latter's excessive leverage in the real estate market.
3. China Food taking over Mengniu Dairy (2319 HK 蒙牛乳業) when the latter suffered scandals related to its milk quality. After acquiring a controlling stake of Mengniu Dairy, China Food took further control of Mengniu's major supplier of fresh milk, China Modern Dairy (1117 HK 現代牧業), and a big marketer and distributor of dairy products in China, Yashili (1230 HK 雅士利國際).

In the meantime, SOE Bright Dairy has made a series of acquisitions at home and abroad. Another major marketer and distributor of dairy products, Ausnutria (1717 HK 澳優乳業), is also likely meat on the table for SOEs.

4. SOE China Resources Gas (1193 HK 華潤燃氣) and China Resources Enterprises (0291 HK 華潤創業) are making a whole range of acquisitions across China.

5. Of the hundreds of acquisitions made so far by the two dominant brewery-sector SOEs, Tsingtao Brewery (0168 HK 青島啤酒股份) and China Resources Brewery Snow, many were from the private sector.

6. State-controlled building materials makers, the sector's dominant players, Anhui Conch (0914 HK 安徽海螺水泥股份), Sinoma (1893 HK 中材股份), and CNBM (3323 HK 中國建材) have made a series of acquisitions, including ones of private sector rivals.

7. State-controlled CIMC taking over Enric (3899 HK 中集安瑞科) and via Enric making more acquisitions.

8. State Pharma Group making lots of acquisitions across the country over the years.

9. China Non-Ferrous Metal Group (8306 HK 中國有色金屬) has made a series of acquisitions in the private sector in recent years.

10. The current downturn in the alternative energy sector (solar and wind power) means that a big number of players in the private sector will become meat for the predatory SOEs.

11
Chapter

Economic Reforms Reversed: The Rise of China's State Sector

PARTY MAN, COMPANY MAN

After Deng Xiaoping came to power in 1978, China's economic reforms focused on two things: deregulation and privatization.

The achievement of these reforms has indeed been remarkable. Many books and articles have discussed that period of history so I will not waste any further space on it. However, what was equally remarkable but less noticed was a significant reversal of the reforms of the past decade.

Let us still focus on two aspects of the reforms: deregulation and privatization. My observations are as follows:

The government has become far more intrusive and overbearing than it was a decade ago. In many areas where rules did not exist, the government has now imposed onerous rules. In other cases where there already were rules, the government has tightened rules to such an extent that many businesses find it hard to breathe.

In the late 1980s, the Chinese government cut the number of ministries from about 100 to about 40 under the leadership of Zhao Zhiyang, the then-Communist Party boss. But the number of new ministries, bureaus, offices, and regulatory bodies has since risen to about 100 again. In the financial industry alone, the four prominent regulatory agencies such as the China Securities Regulatory Commission, the China Insurance Regulatory Commission, the China Banking Regulatory Commission, and the People's Bank of China used to be just one entity: The People's Bank of China. The first three entities were just small parts of the People's Bank when I worked there from 1986 to 1989. While these three new agencies are not officially called "ministries," they are indeed ministry-level agencies. In addition, these agencies are so bloated and the micro-management of their subjects so tedious that I cannot recognize the old People's Bank of China. In what now remains of the People's Bank of China, the number of employees is easily five to six times what it was from 1986 to 1989. Since 2013, I have sat on the board of directors (as an independent director) of a foreign bank incorporated in China. I cannot believe how much the rules have grown.

When I was at the People's Bank of China, the foreign exchange control function of the State Administration of Foreign Exchange (SAFE) was performed by a team of no more than 50 people at the head office, and each provincial and city branch would have at most another 10 people. Today, these numbers have risen to 5 to 10 times that. It is true that today's economy is bigger, but, still, you do not need 10 times the number of people to make monetary policy and 10 times the number of people to monitor foreign exchange movements! In fact, with the help of the internet and computers, the need for regulatory officials should have dramatically declined. In the 1980s, SAFE was an ordinary department of the People's Bank of China. Today, it has been elevated to the place of a vice-ministry-level regulatory body, staffed by thousands of people in total. And China's economic liberalization and foreign exchange deregulation have gone on for more than two decades! The irony is that when Wu Xiaoling became head of SAFE in the early 1990s, she famously said that her wish was to make SAFE redundant. That was the prevailing attitude of ambitious officials at the time. But today, ambitious officials have retreated. Why shouldn't they? The bureaucracy has become so vast, and each official is just a tiny part of it.

When I was at the central bank, I was usually not busy, nor were most of my colleagues. The famous way to describe our work in the office was "a newspaper and a cup of tea." Or we would take a long lunch break coupled with a nap in the office, though many others would choose to play cards for an hour. And we would then almost always take the government shuttle-bus back home at 4:45 in the afternoon.

Today, the newspapers have been swapped for iPhones but my former colleagues now seem visibly busier than I was. Many officials work until late at night, or on the weekends — I never worked weekends in those three years! What, you may ask, are they doing? They are micromanaging the market: approving things, rejecting things, and, very occasionally, extracting "rents." The details they are scrutinizing were things unheard of in my days as a central banker. While close scrutiny does not guarantee getting things right, such scrutiny certainly makes life miserable for the regulated.

Three anecdotes are in order. One is about how much information a company must provide to the securities watchdog if it is going to apply for a listing in the domestic stock market. When I was deputy head of UBS Investment Bank in China, I would always suffer a headache if I had to go and see the watchdog, the China Securities Regulatory Commission. I always tried to shift that duty to my more able and tougher colleagues.

In 2011, after I became chairman of a small microcredit company in Guangzhou, I thought that I would no longer have Big Brother watching over my shoulders. I was wrong. Even my expense reimbursement was linked to the regulatory agency, in real time. It's also worth noting that the regulator in this particular case was the Finance Office at three levels of the government: provincial, city, and district government. I questioned the wisdom of linking all transactions at our small lending company (capitalized at only 27 million U.S. dollars) which is not allowed to take any deposits and which has limited borrowing power. We are allowed to borrow only 50 cents for each dollar of equity we have.

In mid-2013, I was invited to be an independent director of a trust company based in Jiangsu Province — essentially a merchant bank which specialized in the origination and marketing of junk bonds, similar to Michael Milken's Drexel Burnham Lambert in the 1980s to 1990s. I attended a few meetings with the management, and filled out many forms. I liked the opportunity to learn new things. After all, it sounds good to be a board director of a merchant bank. It does not hurt that they would pay me a reasonable sum for a few board meetings per year.

But after too many procedural meetings, I decided to turn down the offer. I was too impatient to deal with the meaningless forms, signatures, and meetings. I wanted something simpler and more interesting.

But despite talk of economic reforms, heightened regulations and increased supervision are everywhere. Many academics criticize the government for having made China "a country of licenses."

Downsized Ministries Still Regulate

In the past two decades, to enhance its reform credentials and to appease critics, the government has transformed many former ministries into "ad hoc" agencies, industry associations, or state-owned enterprises. However, their regulatory functions are still largely intact. For example, the Ministry of Textile Industry was abolished over two decades ago, but the renamed China Textile and Apparel Council has performed residual government functions for the many years that followed.

These days, the Council is still a group of bureaucrats funded by the taxpayers. The Ministry of Petrochemical Industry was renamed China Petrochemical Group (Sinopec), and the Ministry of Petroleum was renamed China National Petroleum Corporation (CNPC), which includes PetroChina. In the power industry, the Ministry of Electric Power was broken down into two power grids and several national power generation companies (such as Huaneng, Datang, and Guodian), and the new regulator is no longer a "ministry," but so what? It is a malfunctioning commission: The China Electricity Supervisory Commission that overlapped and fought turf wars constantly with the Energy Bureau under the National Development and Reform Commission (NDRC).

In March 2013, the Ministry of Railways was abolished and replaced by a General Corporation of Railways. But it was only a change in name. The internal ranks of officials and their regulatory powers have not changed a bit. Coalminers can tell you it is every bit as hard to deal with this "corporation" even if the name has been changed.

Whatever their titles and designations, this much is clear: these entities still perform significant amounts of government functions, still consume taxpayer resources, and bully operators in the same sectors because these entities are generously-funded, have an infinite tolerance for risks, have no pressure to make money, and have almost zero accountability.

According to the Civil Servants Bureau, there were about 7 million civil servants as of the end of 2012. According to the National Bureau of Statistics, however, the number of civil servants in the past decade has risen from just under 11 million to 16.7 million in 2012. If you include those that have been moved to "*shiyedanwei* 事業單位" or "units of official pursuit" (i.e., those entities that are fully funded by the taxpayers but that are not strictly civil servants), the number was around 30 million as of the end of 2012, according to Baidu Zhidao, a public information platform. The wide gap in these figures reflects the restructuring of the civil service and definitions.

In terms of the state ownership of business, it is fair to say that the state sector today is far more dominant than it was a decade ago. While the private sector has grown significantly, the state sector has grown much faster, and particularly in the key areas of banking, finance, real estate, infrastructure, telecoms, pharmaceuticals, healthcare, railways, education, and energy. It is true that the government has sold off a large number of businesses in highly competitive industries but those actions have merely relieved the government of a huge political and financial burden.

From Deregulation to Re-Regulation

It is hard to prove that government regulation has toughened systematically in the past decade. There are claims and counterclaims. Anecdotes, no matter how many you collect, are insufficient to prove a claim. In the Chinese academic and business circles, however, a vast majority seem to agree that the rules have become increasingly more stifling.

I'd like to approach the topic from a different angle. I will compare the outcomes in 2012 and those 10 years earlier. I will analyze tax revenue as a percentage of the GDP in the past two decades. Then I will make some qualitative comparison between the importance of the sectors in the state sector and the private sector. The reason why qualitative analysis is important is because growing numbers of businesses have become difficult to classify as the state sector forms joint ventures with the private sector and because of the stock market's buying and selling.

I will highlight the fact that the two most dominant credit allocation machines in China (the banks and the stock markets) are very heavily skewed in favor of the state sector. It is fair to say that, despite the existence of some hybrid companies, the state sector accounts for over 80% of listed companies weighted by their market-capitalization. Indeed, of the 2000+ listed companies within China there are very few significant private-sector companies, with the exception of perhaps Suning Commerce (the electrical appliance retailer), Yitai Coal, and some real estate developers, for example. Of the 1000+ overseas-listed Chinese companies, the situation looks more encouraging but only slightly so. Over there, there are Tencent, Baidu, and a few other Internet companies, some gas utilities such as ENN, and China Gas, Fosun (conglomerate), some department stores such as Intime, Golden Eagle, and some food processing companies such as Taiwanese-controlled Tingyi, President, and Want Want. Their numbers are below 20. Most other significant companies are all state-controlled, from telecoms, banks, insurers, airlines, ports, toll roads, construction, construction materials, oil, petrochemicals, steel, and metals and mining. Even in hotels and real estate, the state sector has a market share of over one-third, represented by the big players such as China Overseas Land, Vanke, China Resources Land, Sino-Ocean Land, China Merchants Property,

Gemdale, and Greenland.

In terms of bank credit allocation, it is fair to say that over two-thirds go to local and the central governments and commercial entities controlled by them. The three SOEs I served as a director of are good examples.

A Bigger Slice for the Taxman

One way to measure the government's involvement in the economy is to look at the tax revenue as a percentage of GDP over a certain period of time.

My chart below shows that as the economy has been liberalized over the past 35 years, the government has substantially increased its slice of the GDP pie, leading to more income and a healthier balance sheet. The ratio of total fiscal revenue to GDP almost doubled to 22.6% in 2012 from the mid-1990s, on the back of new taxes, higher tax rates, and better collection methods.

Tax revenue as a percentage of GDP in China, 1981–2012

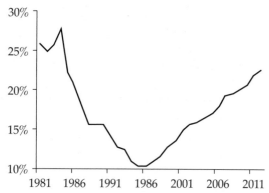

Source: National Bureau of Statistics, China

While much fiscal revenue has been squandered, at least some has been reinvested each year to grow government assets. Today, the government owns controlling stakes in a huge number of banks, telecom operators, ports, roads, railroads, real estate holdings, and industrial companies. Not to mention more than 3 trillion U.S. dollars in foreign government bonds.

A tax is a transfer mechanism. It takes money away from all sectors including the private sector, and gives it to someone else. A large number of new SOEs are created by the infusion of tax revenues, and a large number of existing SOEs receive subsidies and investments from the government.

An Inflation Tax via Bank Credit

This is how it works. The banks (all owned and controlled by the state, with the exception of the mid-sized Minsheng Bank whose 3 trillion yuan in total deposits accounted for about 3% of the banking industry's total deposits as of the end of 2013) had limited amounts of funds to lend. The central bank assured the banks not to worry. The People's Bank of China is supposed to be "the lender of last resort." But its role has always been "the lender of first resort." At the beginning of every year starting from the early 1980s, all the banks would have a forecast of how much their deposits would be and how much their outstanding loans would be in the course of the year. For example, Bank A wanted to achieve an average loan balance of 100 million yuan in 1986, but its expected deposit balance was likely to be 80 million yuan. Was that an issue? No. Ask the central bank for a loan to plug the gap! At the time, I was at the central bank, and I was familiar with that bargaining, not just in the Annual Bank Conference in mid-December, but also in the countless smoky boardroom meetings. It was a common scene in the narrow and dark corridors of the People's Bank of China: a mayor or a governor from some province would patiently sit there and wait for an opportunity to lobby my colleagues for a bigger loan ration for his jurisdiction. Even junior officers like me had been subject to intense lobbying.

Instead of lending out 60% or 70% of their total deposits, the Chinese banks had often lent out more than 100% — more than they took in as deposits! How could that have been possible? Where had the extra loans come from? They had come from the central bank's printing press, of course!

Strictly speaking, a bank does not need deposits before lending out money, as long as the borrower puts the borrowed money back into the bank as deposits. In other words, the bank can extend a loan before taking in a deposit.

See the chart below. The banking sector's loan-to-deposit ratios have been well above 100% for a long time.

Loan-to-deposit ratio of the Chinese banking sector, 1978–2012

Source: People's Bank of China and National Bureau of Statistics, China

The data above is no secret, and it is from the National Bureau of Statistics and the People's Bank of China. Extraordinarily high loan-to-deposit ratios were common in the 1970s through the 1990s. That situation lasted for almost two decades. From about 2000 to 2001, together with the massive re-capitalization of the banking sector, the government brought down the loan-to-deposit ratios. But we must remember two things. First, the extra money released by the aggressive work of the printing press in the two previous decades had not disappeared just because many loans had gone bust. Indeed, the purchasing power created had stayed in the economy and it had just changed hands. Second, the "moderation" of the loan-to-deposit ratio since 2000 was no moderation at all. The banking industry from 2000 to 2003 had received a massive recapitalization. The big boost to the banks' equity capital base immediately became new loans which, in turn, became new deposits. So, even with a much more modest loan-to-deposit ratio, the total credit balance in the economy jumped quickly right after the recapitalization of 2000. See the thinner line in the chart below. The chart below shows the growth rates of deposits and outstanding loans.

Growth of deposits and outstanding loans, 2000–2004

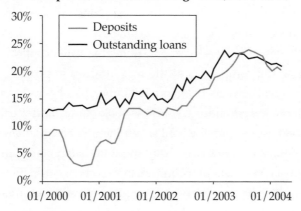

Source: Wind Information

It was not unusual in the 1980s and even the 1990s for a bank to suddenly find itself "stuck." In other words, it had lent out so much that it simply did not have money to meet depositors' withdrawals. In that situation, the central bank had to step in to provide emergency loans. Emergency loans had soon become commonplace, and some banks eventually used the tactic to force more loans from the central bank. Although these banks had received a slap on their wrists, the benefits of bad behavior were so enormous that some banks would do it again and again. As some bankers and local politicians would jokingly say, "The thrill justified the sin."

PARTY MAN, COMPANY MAN

The rapid growth of total loans since the early 1980s, coupled with lax loan standards, resulted in ratios of 30% to 40% of non-performing loans by the late 1990s.

In 1999 to 2000, the Chinese government staged a massive re-capitalization program. The funds for the recapitalization came from both the Ministry of Finance (tax revenues) and the printing presses of the central bank. The size of the re-capitalization was so massive that it contributed to the high inflation in subsequent years. In addition, the government floated the banks in the domestic and Hong Kong stock exchanges one after another – sucking in trillions in new capital. Subsequent to the floatation, the banks raised considerable additional capital through retained (undistributed) profits, sales of new shares, convertible bonds, and preference shares. All these resources have come under the state's control.

Despite the complexity of the recapitalization process, this much is clear: Between 1999 and 2005, the "bad banks" — asset management corporations (AMCs) — took out around 2 trillion yuan of bad assets from the banks, and injected an equal amount of fresh equity into them. In 2000, the total loan balance in the industry was less than 10 trillion yuan. In other words, in those few years, the banks received an equity injection equivalent to more than 20% of their loan balance! It was like suddenly giving the banks a 20%-plus capital adequacy ratio, more than twice required, on top of whatever they already had at the time. Imagine how much expansionary and inflationary power the industry had suddenly gained with the stroke of a few pens!

Where did the fresh equity come from? Part of it came from the Ministry of Finance and part from the central bank's lending to the AMCs (i.e., the printing press). Indeed, it did not matter where the money came from, as the addition to the credit expansion capability was the same.

The government's budget deficit in 1999 was 174 billion yuan and in 2000 it was 250 billion yuan. While these were only 2% to 3% of GDP, they were 15% to 19% of the total budgets at the time.

How then did the Ministry of Finance find the money to prop up the banks without bankrupting the government? Easy. They let the printing press do the heavy lifting. In 2000, the Ministry of Finance wrote an IOU to the AMCs worth 40 billion yuan and this "promise" enabled the AMCs to borrow 634 billion yuan from the central bank. Of course, even that 40 billion yuan was unnecessary. Who in the world would question — let alone be able to stop — the central bank from lending to the empty AMCs, whatever the amount?

Even if the recapitalization had been entirely funded by the Ministry of Finance, it would have been the same as resorting to the printing press of the central bank. First of all, fiscal spending is nowhere nearly as powerful as the banks' capital which has a multiplying effect on the creation of credit. Second, whatever the theoretical distinctions, it is practically impossible to separate the Ministry of Finance and the central bank, particularly in China. Both are departments under the State Council, the cabinet. In response to the total insolvency of the banks, the central bank aggressively cut interest rates from 1997 to 2000. The cuts fell more heavily on the deposit rates (by 549 basis points) than on the lending side (by 477 basis points). See chart below.

Interest rates for fixed-term saving and term loans, 1990–2010

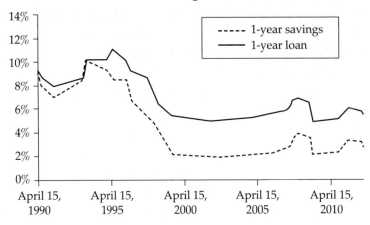

Source: People's Bank of China

But this widening of the banks' interest rate spread understated the actual benefits to the banks: The much lower *absolute level* of the interest rates pushed loan growth back up in subsequent years — 13% in 2001, 17% in 2002, and 21% in 2003 — despite an ever-higher base. The additional loans generated huge sales tax and dividends for the Ministry of Finance.

In the 1990s, the whole banking sector had been loss-making thanks to high inflation, inflation-linked deposit rates, low lending rates, and a high number of bad loans. But after 2000, that changed dramatically. The newly-minted fat profits enabled the banks to pay taxes (and dividends) to the Ministry of Finance, which then helped recapitalize the banks in rights issues in subsequent years.

Additionally, since 2000, the central bank has kept interest rates on deposits very low (and often below inflation) to reduce the coupon rates on Treasury bonds that are priced against deposit rates.

Of course, the central bank did a few things here and there to reduce the expansionary power of the monstrous recapitalization from 2000 to 2003, such as imposing lending quotas, and raising reserve requirement ratios to over 20%! But even these dramatic measures were not enough to neutralize the power of the additional "high powered" money in the banks. We have seen a credit explosion since then. The banks' subsequent IPOs, rights issues, convertible bonds, block trades, and retained earnings have given the banks even more firepower, pushing loan growth since 2000 back up to a 16.6% compound annual rate.

In conclusion, since 1999 to 2000, the government has increased the size of the banking industry through a combination of (1) recapitalization of the banks, (2) public listings (IPOs) of the banks, (3) additional fund-raisings (such as the selling of new shares) for the banks, or (4) artificial controls over interest rates (which gives the banks a guaranteed and fat profit margin). As a result of these measures, and the rapid loan growth for 13 years, the banking sector now accounts for almost half of all the profits in the stock market, and if we include the oil and gas sector (which was predominantly controlled by the government), the state sector's share of net profits in all listed companies has been 70% to 85%! See table below.

The state-controlled banks alone account for over half of the profits in the whole economy. The interest rate controls rip off everyone else to enrich the banks.

Sectoral share of net profits in China's listed companies, 2005–2012

	2005	2007	2009	2010	2011	2012
All listed companies (million CNY)	531,554	1,162,532	1,306,367	1,822,376	2,064,744	2,080,492
Finance (% of total)	29.6	37.7	46.5	43.2	46.6	53.0
Oil and gas (% of total)	33.3	46.5	28.7	29.5	23.6	18.4
Finance plus oil and gas (% of total)	62.9	84.2	75.3	72.6	70.2	71.4

Source: Wind Information

If the table above is not enough to shock, I do not know what is. For those who say that the state sector is losing battles to the private sector, this table is an uncomfortable reminder of reality.

In the unlisted universe, there are a few big national banks such as China Development Bank, and China Postal Bank. In addition, there are thousands of city commercial banks and rural commercial banks that are owned and controlled by the state.

Let's try an analogy.

Before the recapitalization of the banks in 2000 to 2003, the relative share of the economy between the state sector and the private sector was, say, 70% to 30%. After the recapitalization, the ratio has become, say, 85% to 15%. This is similar to the controlling shareholder of a publicly-listed company diluting the stakes of the minority shareholders. In China, this dilution takes place through the central bank's printing press (and to a lesser extent, the tax revenues).

How to Abuse Performance Data

Nicholas Lardy, in a recent Bloomberg Brief piece, compared the financial performance of China's state sector with the private sector. Citing the National Bureau of Statistics, his numbers were predictable: in 2012, the state sector ROA (return on assets) was merely 4.6% which was well below the private sector's 12.4%.

But I think those numbers are biased and wrong.

Why? The biggest components of the state sector are the banks which account for almost half of the domestic stock market valuation, and about half of the total net profits of all the listed companies. Other big components in the stock market — or in the unlisted universe for that matter — are state-controlled big insurance companies, big oil corporations, and telecom operators. The Chinese banks have an average ROE of about 20% and that's twice the level of their global peers. Insurance companies do well in general, and telecom operators enjoy exorbitant privileges. How can the state sector underperform the private sector in financial terms?

Of course, you can argue that the banks' profits are entirely due to the government's control on interest rates. That is a true and fair assessment in my view. But the fact of the matter is that the state sector has much higher ROEs than the private sector.

Lardy cleverly used ROA in his graph. That is meaningless because banks are the most highly-geared business, and their ROAs are low in nature (say, 2% to 3%). But the nature of the banking business is such that you cannot compare banking with other sectors on ROAs. ROE is the right benchmark.

The other problem with Lardy's performance comparison between the state and private sectors is that thousands and thousands of private sector companies go bankrupt or voluntarily shut down each year. Once that happens, they exit from the statistics. So there is a "survival basis." This is as meaningless as the hedge fund sector's performance data. But you hear of no SOE being shut down. The state sector not only benefits from the economies of scale, but also from the economies of scope. The state sector as a whole is like a giant conglomerate company that benefits from diversification, the low cost of plentiful funding, and political favors. The playing field is unfair and aligned against the private sector.

It is meaningless to compare the financial performance between SOEs and their private sector rivals, as the playing field is unfair and aligned against the private sector.

Finally, the state sector takes on many social functions and their existence and activities provide a positive spillover effect for the whole economy and society. While liberal commentators may disagree with this, the state sector is designed to achieve more than just financial ratios. For example, in all utilities (power, water, natural gas, and public transportation) in China, the state sector dominates, and in these asset-heavy sectors, the operators do not charge a full price because of affordability and other social reasons. That drags down their financial returns, but the financial ratios do not reflect their efficiency.

Sadly, it is wrong for liberal economists to say that the dominance of the state sector goes against the public's wishes. In China, the public wants more, not less, involvement by the state sector. The public wants a bigger state sector to tackle the many challenges China faces, even if many of these challenges are byproducts of the state sector (inequality, overpopulation, and pollution).

Even the recent Third Plenum does not mention the private sector, a point even Lardy acknowledges.

The official data shows that the government tax revenue as a percentage of GDP almost doubled from 12% a decade ago to 22% in 2012. This is almost a wholesale reversal of the economic liberalization of the previous two decades. But Western economists do not mention this uncomfortable fact.

The writing is on the wall: the score of the past decade's match of the private sector vs. the state sector in China is "private sector zero" and "state sector one."

The newfound economic leverage of the state sector in China can be seen in the money being spent on new infrastructure projects by the government. In the last three decades, China has built thousands of kilometers of new highways, and countless tunnels and bridges. When I worked at the central bank in the 1980s, there were only 4 bridges over the Yangtze River. Today, there are 86 bridges and tunnels. In 1986, I travelled from Guangzhou to Shenzhen for business. That was a full day's job; the bumpy road was muddy and paved only with pebbles. There were potholes and unexpected delays due to the poor condition of the highway. Today, the trip takes about 90 minutes despite routine traffic jams. That trip will be even faster during off-peak hours.

The quantum leap in infrastructure is visible not only in the eastern coastal provinces but also even in central Hubei, and further inland in Sichuan Province. There, the highways are top quality ones even by global standards. Many road builders are still losing money and financial returns will be questionable in the foreseeable future. But these projects, like highways, are essential and hugely helpful in lifting millions out of poverty, and creating new business opportunities.

And take a guess who is taking risks in building these roads and highways? The state sector, of course. Most of the local government debt (some 18 trillion yuan, or 3 trillion U.S. dollars, according to the central government's audit office) that the capital market frets about has gone to these projects (roads, tunnels, airports, and other infrastructure projects).

It is impossible for the private sector to even contemplate this type of big project. They have neither the financial resources, nor the risk appetite. I will go one step further and argue that they do not have the organizing expertise. After all, China's private sector remains a very young and — dare I say it? — poorly-organized force.

The state sector's fortress of power over the economy is ringed by a wall of strategically important sectors — essential infrastructure (like roads) and sectors with pricing power — while the private sector is now left outside trying to claw its way in via the fiercely competitive dead-end sectors like low-end manufacturing, retail businesses, service industries, and (some) real estate. The state sector's position seems invulnerable and one can guess that an investor like Warren Buffett would have put his money in those industries which the state sector has cleverly chosen to hoard and retain.

There is a difference between our wishes and reality.

12
Chapter

They Love the State
Sector, Honestly

In China, the officials and general public admire the United States, even if they do not necessarily want to follow the U.S. ways of doing things.

In the past two decades, I have worked for several European banks in various capacities. As an analyst, I would study China stocks and then later work on deals between the Chinese government and the European companies. These banks included UBS, HSBC, and CLSA. Through my work, I came to see that the Chinese people admire and love America but many hate and envy the country at the same time. At UBS, when I would pitch a deal to a Chinese government entity or business, they would usually prefer to hire an American bank if the terms were similar. In other words, I had to work harder to win deals. I asked some of my friends in China and they confirmed this bias.

The U.S. dominance in the world means that the country has a disproportionate influence on global ideology and policies. Two recent events in the U.S. have had considerable influence and will continue to influence Chinese public opinion: the U.S. government's handling of the subprime crisis and the U.S. government shutdown in October 2013.

In many ways, the battles between the Democrats and Republicans in the U.S. on healthcare, the budget deficit ceiling, taxes, the Federal Reserve's Quantitative Easing, and the Troubled Asset Relief Program (TARP) have all been fascinating to watch.

The Chinese public's curiosity about U.S. policy struggles is largely due to the perception of the Chinese that the U.S. is the champion of the principles of a free market economy. But many recent events suggest to the Chinese that even the champion may not be so free after all.

Alan Greenspan, the former Chairman of the Federal Reserve for 19 years, had often eloquently defended the Federal Reserve's hands-off policies on financial markets. His testimony to Congress on mortgages in general, and subprime mortgages in particular, and his robust defense of the explosive growth of the derivatives market all made a strong impression on the Chinese observers. But the subsequent subprime crisis proved that Greenspan was wrong to leave the market alone.

On another front, most Chinese believed that the U.S. Fed was only responsible to Congress, not the executive branch of the government, and that the independence of the Fed was a cardinal rule of the U.S. financial system. In the meantime, the Chinese generally believe that their own central bank, the People's Bank of China — a part of the State Council, the government — is an inferior system.

When the Fed started to provide unlimited liquidity to the banks, and when TARP and then Quantitative Easing were announced, many Chinese commentators were taken aback. "My God, we have misunderstood the U.S. Fed." Or "Aha! The U.S. central bank and the Department of the Treasury are one and the same! Their structure is no different from the Chinese ones. The only difference is that they pretend to be independent. We do not even pretend!"

When the U.S. government bailed out Bear Sterns, General Motors, Citigroup, and the two housing-market giants (Fannie Mae and Freddie Mac), and when the British government nationalized RBS and several other banks, the strenuous cries of "This is not a bailout" from politicians rang hollow in China. The Chinese officials felt hugely relieved because this showed that what we normally do in China was nothing extraordinary after all! Many champions of the free market in the Chinese government and academia were not only embarrassed but they also retreated from their positions. As a result, some criticized the West for applying a double standard on China. For example, some commentators argued that China's handling of the yuan's exchange rates and the cross-border capital mobility were entirely rational and legitimate. Even in the West, the Chinese intervention and refusal to open up the market gained more recognition. Ha-Joon Chang, reader of economics at Cambridge University, and

Hélène Rey, Professor of Economics at London Business School, both believe that restricting capital movements is sensible for developing countries.

What was astonishing to Chinese officials and the public was that, when a large number of free market believers in Chinese academia criticized the government's 4 trillion yuan economic stimulus program in late 2008 in response to the failure of Lehman Brothers, Western politicians and the media, almost without exception, praised the Chinese action, despite their free market bias and frequent criticism of the Chinese government's intervention in the economy. This sharp contrast continued in the years since. For example, Nicholas Lardy of the Peterson Institute for International Economics, in his 2013 book, *Sustaining China's Economic Growth After the Global Financial Crisis*, praised China's response to the global slowdown as timely and necessary. Former U.S. Treasury Secretary Hank Paulson also made similar complimentary remarks.

Following the global crisis, the interventionist factions among economists gained an upper hand in China. Popular anti-free market books, such as *23 Things They Don't Tell You About Capitalism* by Ha-Joon Chang, Mariana Mazzucato's *The Entrepreneurial State: Debunking Public vs. Private Sector Myths*, and Ian Bremmer's *The End of the Free Market: Who Wins the War Between States and Corporations?* are now widely talked about among Chinese researchers and policymakers. Keynesian theories have also become more fashionable, as Paul Krugman's books and articles have been translated into many languages including Chinese.

The subprime crisis in the U.S. and the banking crisis in Europe play into the hands of interventionist ideologues in China.

In essence, China's 4 trillion yuan economic stimulus program and the U.S. QE program have had the same effect on aggregate demand and monetary expansion. What is different is that the U.S. government refrains from directly operating businesses, while the Chinese program has led to the creation of many government-owned businesses. We can also justify these massive policy actions as exceptions, but where do we draw the policy line? And how exceptional a circumstance is exceptional enough?

Praying for a Major Slowdown in China

In the last quarter [Q42013], China's economic growth slowed to 7.7%, the weakest since 2009. And the market is very concerned about it. But as a loyal Chinese citizen and a private investor, I pray for a further slowdown, and a significant one.

It is no secret that China's high growth in the past 35 years has been spurred by aggressive fiscal and monetary stimulation, as well as higher productivity. For example, in the past 27 years, China's bank credit has expanded at a compound annual rate of 18%, and money supply at 21%. Alongside the high growth of economic activities, a large array of ills has popped up and some of these are unbearable: environmental catastrophe; resources depletion; income inequality; and runaway government debt. Indeed, all these ills are interlinked.

But how would I like the economy to slow? I'd like the government to liberate the prices of at least three things: utilities, money, and currency.

First of all, I want to see tariffs on water, gas, and electricity rise substantially — by as much as two to three times immediately, if possible.

Do you think I am being aggressive? I'm not. In the past decade, or two or three, the prices of utilities have lagged far behind inflation and this has led to huge amounts of waste, pollution, and depletion of resources. Despite condemnation by the government and the public, most of the heavy polluters continue to operate because they extract "environmental dividends" from the planet without paying an adequate price. If, as I expect, many big polluters were to shut down, contributing to an economic recession, that would be a welcome change.

Second, in most of the past 35 years, China's interest rates on bank deposits have not reflected the sacrifice of the savers who are delaying private consumption. And, indeed, those deposits have been below the inflation rate. That rip-off has led to huge and persistent subsidies to business. Sadly, the low interest rates on loans have meant low hurdle rates of returns on investments. That has artificially boosted economic activity for too long.

Finally, whatever your school of thought, the most undisputed test of a currency's fair exchange rate has to be the actual outcome which is the trade balances of a country in the medium and long term. The fact that China has run a trade surplus of a large magnitude in the past two decades proves the point. The mainstream view is that this currency distortion benefits China, but I do not believe that it does. It is nothing but unfavorable terms of trade against China. In addition to extra transaction costs associated with currency controls, it amounts to a reduction of Chinese consumers' real incomes, particularly in terms of the quantities of imported goods they can purchase. It is a subsidy the household sector is forced to provide to businesses. It depresses private consumption. And it is a rip-off.

They say that if something is not sustainable, it will stop. China's rapid growth, fuelled by fiscal and monetary stimulus policies, will stop. The only questions are when and how. Given the dominance of the state sector that has a high tolerance for low returns, and the existence of millions of low-wage workers, *China Inc.'s* business model can continue for a long while. But that does not mean that prolonging the status quo is in the best interest of China's citizenry. The sooner the economy slows on the back of higher utilities tariffs, higher interest rates, and a higher exchange rate for the yuan, the better it will be for the country.

A sharp slowdown in the economy does not mean weak returns for equity investors. This was shown by the U.S. experience.

In an essay published in 2001, Warren Buffett split the 34 years between 1964 and 1998 into two equal periods. In the first

17 years, the U.S. economy surged a cumulative 373%, while the Dow ended flat, hovering mostly at around 875 points in that period. In the second 17-year period, however, while the economy grew by a modest 177%, the Dow staged a 10-fold surge, from 875 points to 9,181!

Why the contradiction? Warren Buffett was not trying to prove that GDP (or GNP) was negatively correlated to equity returns. However, his message was loud and clear: in the long run, it was the inflation rate (and thus nominal interest rates) that mattered to equity valuations and, therefore, returns. In the first 17-year period, yields on long-term government bonds surged from 4.2% to 13.7% on the back of rising inflation. However, in the second 17-year period, the yields fell steadily from 13.7% to 5.1%, thanks to the tough monetary policy of then-Chairman of the Federal Reserve, Paul Volker.

You cannot find a better response to the experience of the U.S. than China today. In the past two decades, investors in China equities got a lousy deal — both the domestic stock market and the H-shares markets disappointed hugely — despite double-digit real growth of the economy year after year. The reasons included poor corporate governance, and the rapid dilution of shareholder interests. More importantly, high inflation and therefore high nominal interest rates in the free market — though not the regulated interest rates — have hurt corporate profitability and the valuation of equities.

In a counter-intuitive way, China must raise interest rates to eventually bring down interest rates, via the conquering of inflation.

So that is why I pray for a further slowdown of the Chinese economy.

Good People, Bad Government

When I was a kid in China in the 1960s and 1970s, I often heard official propaganda about the imperialism of the U.S. and its desire to rule the world. "The American people are good but it is just that their government is bad," or so went the Chinese propaganda.

But is the U.S. government not publicly elected? "Oh, those elections are just the results of the fighting of money machines, and the results are heavily manipulated. The American public is brutally oppressed and their views are different from their government's positions."

After I left China in early 1989, I discovered that the views of those in the West about China are sometimes equally naïve and simplistic. They argue that the Chinese government has no legitimacy because it is not publicly elected. They say that the Chinese Communist Party is hated by the public. But sadly, that is not true. When it comes to economic policy, one would be surprised how much public discussion and debate there is in the public domain: through print media, TV, and the Internet. Criticism (and very harsh criticism) of government policies is everywhere. In fact, I would say that most economic policies in China seem to have the support of the majority of the public.

China does not have a federal-state system. Despite the presence of regional and local parliaments (congress), the truth is that the governments of provinces, cities, counties, and towns are strictly branches of the central government. These regional and local governments have their own (minor) taxes and levies and also share some tax revenues with the central government. But the central government decides the revenue sharing formula, and redistributes some revenue between regions and cities. So, regional and local governments do not really have independent finances to speak of. Legally, regional and local governments do not have the right to raise funds through the bond market. But in many cases, the central government sells bonds on behalf of regional and local governments, and ultimately stands behind all regional and local governments. This is very different from the U.S. federal-state system under which Orange County in

California or the city of Detroit declared bankruptcy while the rest of the country looked on.

Until the mid-1990s, working for an SOE (state-owned enterprise) such as Shenzhen Investment or China Telecom was the same as working for a government department. The wages, benefits, and pensions were similar. However, this became untenable in the 1990s and the government split the civil service from the state sector (SOEs). Gradually, this meant that the head of a SOE could make 10 times or 20 times more than their political masters (for example, ministers). Of course, it also meant that they could make much less (though this has been a rare occurrence so far). In most cases, employees at a bankrupt SOE would be redeployed to another SOE.

There are other differences between the civil service and SOEs. The SOE jobs may not be permanent, and their pensions are lower. In fact, the civil service and SOEs are covered by different pension plans.

What about state ownership of the economy? Many in the West may think that China's ruling class has imposed state capitalism upon the masses and that they have no option but to tolerate it. That is not true. If there were a referendum on state ownership today, I bet the overwhelming majority would vote for the status quo, or a variation of it. I also think they would vote to reject wholesale privatization, or any substantial move in that direction. I would even

> **//Contrary to the perception in the West, the Chinese public wants a bigger, not a smaller, state sector. //**

speculate that many would want the government to play a bigger role in the economy. In other words, the government policies more or less reflect the public's wishes, despite a lack of democracy. We may not like to hear this, but it is a reality.

Will China become a democracy as a result of the ongoing economic liberalization? The prevailing view in the West is that the private sector is winning market share against the bloated state sector left, right, and center. The mainstream Western view is that the private sector is morally right, operationally more efficient, and should easily crush the state sector in China, and that Western-style democracy is a foregone conclusion. But as I have described earlier in the book, the state sector in China is actively adapting to a new environment — and doing so remarkably well — and that, in fact, there has been a significant reversal on the market share for the state sector in the past decade (since about 2001 to 2002).

Each time there is a crisis (such as an oil spill along the coast, an explosion of gas pipes, a food poisoning case at a school, corporate fraud, or a power brownout), the Chinese public will call for tighter regulation, and more stringent surveillance. And the government would soon react accordingly. But few have realized that regulation leads to regulation, and the result is a stifling system that kills business. Indeed, I see that happening in the U.S. and Europe, too.

In my other book, *Inside China's Shadow Banking: The Next Subprime Crisis?*, I chronicled my experiences running a microcredit company in Guangzhou, and my frustration at dealing with regulators at the district, city, and provincial government levels. The microcredit industry is indeed overly regulated. But which sector is not tightly regulated in China? I lobbied and campaigned aggressively for the government to relax some unnecessary and harmful rules, and wrote many essays and gave many public speeches hoping to win public support. In the end, I found that the tight regulation was not "just the result of a few unsympathetic idiots sitting in air conditioned government offices." Rather, I came to figure out that the system has broad public support, however unwise and ill-informed I may think the public are.

Maybe they are all right and rational, while I am the stupid idiot that is making a fuss? Whatever the case, the reality is the reality. I am not trying to pass judgment on whether the free market works or not. I am simply making the point that state capitalism is here to stay, and for a long time to come. In other words, this book is not about what I think China should do to its state capitalism, but what I think it will do.

For ideological reasons, the West thinks that democracy and freedom of choice will win in the end. When such an outcome doesn't seem forthcoming, those in the West jump to another conclusion that China will descend into chaos and an economic depression and financial collapse, as Gordon G. Chang predicted in his famous — now infamous, perhaps — book, *The Coming Collapse of China*.

The Public Wants a Bigger Government

Libertarians religiously believe that since the government is only a necessary evil, its size should be contained to the very minimum. They further believe that since the Chinese people are rational that they will demand democracy as soon as possible.

While I do not have a strong preference on either libertarian or authoritarian values, I can only describe what I see matter of factly.

It is obvious to the vast majority of the Chinese people that the country's poverty is due — at least in part — to overpopulation. Those in the West also say the same thing about the Asian subcontinent and Africa.

Let us look at the sensitive issue of China's population control methods. Those in the West condemn China's attempts at population control, and the one-child policy, but what they do not understand is that the official policy has overwhelming support inside China. To many in the West, this is an inconvenient truth. But the West and academia have a way of ignoring the fact that these population control methods by China's government are aimed (somewhat) at alleviating poverty.

PARTY MAN, COMPANY MAN

In the 1950s and 1960s, millions of Chinese died of starvation because of political upheaval and poor agricultural productivity, as well as a population explosion. Overpopulation had become the number one policy challenge even before Mao's death. So, population controls were introduced, and gradually tightened, and eventually a strict "one-child policy" was introduced in the 1980s. There was resistance from many citizens in those years, but I dare say, there has been growing support from citizens in the past two decades. You may ask, what is the basis for such an assertion?

> **// The one-child policy has many flaws, but it is not without popular support. //**

The problem of overpopulation was evident, and anyone with common sense was able to see it. The government's policy was for the common good and those who opposed the policy only (or mainly) wanted the policy relaxed on themselves, but not on others. So it was more a selfish desire to be treated more equally than others were being treated.

You cannot imagine a policy that affected millions of families to last for over four decades without the backing of the majority of the public. By the same token, you cannot imagine the overthrow of the Nationalist KMT government by the Communist Party without public support, and without millions of ordinary souls willing to sacrifice their own lives for the cause.

Equally, you cannot imagine the political chaos in the Cultural Revolution to be just Mao's crazy ideology, rather than the collective madness of the Chinese majority. It is all too easy to say that the public had been intoxicated by the government's systematic brainwashing. But who was the government? You cannot imagine the government to be made up of just a few diehard evildoers in such a big country.

Many Western observers criticize the Chinese Communist Party for not abandoning the Mao doctrine and still holding Chairman Mao in high esteem. My reading of the situation is very different: It is not only that the Party is holding Mao in high esteem, but also the Chinese public who are doing the same. Fully aware of the disasters Mao brought to China in the 1950s and up to the 1970s, the Chinese public see themselves in Mao. Mao was one of them, and the crystallization of their wishes for a leader. The Chinese always want to have a leader, and want to be governed. As part of human nature, it is always the most difficult task to criticize ourselves. This is what the Chinese public has refused to do so far. But they will eventually do it, albeit after a very long delay. Even when their behavior in the past three decades completely contradicted Mao's ideology, they still refrain from admitting as much.

In the meantime, the majority of the Chinese public sees a powerful state sector as their compass and emotional assurance. The state is the savior of the people in China.

Furthermore, it is analytically flawed to claim that today's growing dominance of the state sector in China has no political, social, or cultural backing. The flaws of the state sector are out there in the open for everyone to see, and are widely documented, blasted, and hated. But the state sector is not just surviving but prospering. You cannot dismiss it as the irrational brainchild of a few top politicians, or blame it on the stupidity of the public.

Before I became Chairman of Wansui, the microcredit business in Guangzhou, I had always thought that the regulatory officials were stupid and were working against the public's wishes and the public interest. They made rules so stifling for the microcredit industry that I strongly believed that they were wrong.

Having tirelessly lobbied for policy change, having got to know these regulatory officials personally, and having spoken with many ordinary citizens in the course of those two years, I had to concede that the regulations were just what the public wanted at that juncture. As I wrote in my book, *Inside China's Shadow Banking: The Next Subprime Crisis?*, even though I, out of self-righteousness, believe that the regulations are against the public interest, I cannot say it is against the public's wishes. Who am I to tell others, in a condescending way, that they are hurting their own self-interest?

Coming back to the subject of population controls: my elder sister, Yuqing, now 62 years old, and her husband had their flour-milling business shut down by the Maliang government after their second child, Dongqing, was born in 1986. That was their only business and they suffered enormously as a result of the punishment. At the time I was at the central bank in Beijing, and an influential celebrity in Maliang, my hometown. But it had never occurred to me that I should have lobbied the town government to reduce the punishment for my sister. I dared not, as the policy was so strict and the popular sentiment was so strongly in favor of the policy.

Tied to concerns about overpopulation are worries about overconsumption. The issues are linked.

Consumptionnomics: Asia's Role in Reshaping Capitalism and Saving the Planet, by Chandran Nair, is a decent book. In it, the author sharply criticized Western countries for preaching energy conservation to developing countries, but those same Western countries are unwilling to take responsibility for their past. He also blasted the West for preaching higher consumption to developing countries without considering the consequences of higher consumption on global resource constraints and the environment. However, in such a detailed work, the author mysteriously neglected to mention, even in passing, let alone properly analyze, the biggest challenge to the global environment and resources: overpopulation. A coincidence? Self-censorship for fear of offending the mainstream?

While Nair and others stress their alternative strategy to the growth-based approach to development, I wonder if there is an alternative at all, given the vast difference between goals of materialistic attainment in the West and countries like China and India. If the government of India or China were to push for an "alternative" strategy at the expense of materialistic growth, they will quickly lose political legitimacy and see themselves thrown out of office. Mao Zedong of China pursued an alternative strategy, albeit a different alternative strategy, only to see China slide into starvation and political chaos. Is there another alternative? I do not think so. The former Chinese leader Deng Xiaoping, cleverly asserted that, "Development is the key (*yingdaoli* 硬道理)." Here, Deng meant "materialistic growth" when he said "development." Soon after Deng uttered these words, they were made a dominant strategy of the government after 1992.

Taking overpopulation and unstoppable population growth as givens, Nair advocated a Spartan and austere way of life for Asian countries based on sacrifice and restraint. This is spiritually honorable perhaps, but practically impossible to implement. As Nair himself acknowledged in his book, "if a major Asian country — China, say, or India — were unilaterally to impose a stiff carbon and resources tax on imports, it could find itself embroiled in trade clashes with Europe and America that would undermine cooperation on other issues." True. But does Nair think the domestic constituencies in India or China easier to convince?

Human beings respond to price signals. If it is impractical for poor Asian countries to levy carbon taxes on imports, is it possible for them to impose higher domestic taxes? Surely, the domestic businesses would protest the loss of competitiveness against other countries. Is a globally coordinated policy feasible?

When China started its economic reforms three decades ago, the West often predicted that India would outperform China in economic terms due to India's language advantage, its robust democracy, and its efficient private sector. But three decades later, we see big gaps the other way round. Today, if you were to poll the same academics and Western officials, chances are they still hold their stubborn views, not allowing facts to get in the way of a good story. It is true that China has major and even intractable problems, but does India not have more difficult issues to deal with (overpopulation being one of them)?

Addressing environmental issues and inequality both require a strong government. A big state sector is one way (albeit not the only way, and not necessarily the most efficient way) to deal with these challenges. Until a credible policy replacement is in place, the existing state sector is here to stay and may grow in significance.

In an op-ed in *The Wall Street Journal*, Nicholas Eberstadt at the American Enterprise Institute blasted the Chinese government's cruel and inhumane policy on population control. Citing authoritative analysis and estimates, he warned of a demographic crash in China due to the one-child policy. He wrote:

> Demographers at the United Nations Population Division and the U.S. Census Bureau calculate that Chinese fertility levels today are far below the level necessary for population replacement. By their reckonings, current childbearing patterns, if continued, would mean each successive generation would shrink by 25% (UNPD) or 27% (Census Bureau). Official Chinese estimates, and the work of some independent Chinese demographers, suggest an even steeper drop.

I am no demographer, and cannot judge the analysis cited above. However, I dare say that, in my best judgment, the one-child policy has wide public support. If the support was narrow-based two decades ago, it is certainly broad-based today. In my view, it is not true to say that the one-child policy is the brainchild of a few die-hard Communist Party elders and their ruthless ideologues. I am disturbed as much as Western critics about the harsh implementation of the one-child policy in some instances, but there is no denying that overpopulation is a central issue for the environment, prosperity, and even social harmony of China and other countries. Inconvenient as though this may sound, I think the decline of the population is what the Chinese government (with the public support) is aiming at.

The point I am making is that, short of democracy, public policies such as the one-child policy and the state sector dominance, command wide social support. It is incorrect to claim that the big state sector had been imposed by the "ruling class" onto the public that did not have a choice. Outsiders — and, indeed, many insiders — may judge that some policies are detrimental to China's self-interest, but that is what you get in a democracy as well.

Does the Public Have a Say in the Choice of the State Sector?

For sure, China is not a democracy in the Western sense. But freedom of speech is exercised widely, due in part to the proliferation of the Internet. Around half of the citizenry uses the Internet regularly, and probably up to 90% have access to it. It is acceptable for anyone — even senior politicians themselves — to criticize publicly any government policy (even outside their own portfolio of responsibility) with the exception of core political issues such as the one-party rule. Browsing the Chinese Internet, and even the official newspapers, shows that there are only a few "no-fly zones" on the Internet in China.

In fact, this is not new. Even in the 1980s, well before the Internet visited China, freedom of speech was widely enjoyed by the public, contrary to perceptions in the West. One small event serves to illustrate the point. When I was a junior officer at the central bank in Beijing in 1986 to 1989, I often criticized economic policies in my articles in the official media.

On September 8, 1988, the State Council, China's cabinet, promulgated a law regulating the use of cash in business transactions. The main idea was to force large transactions into bank transfers and check accounts, instead of using cash. The law was named *Interim Regulations on Cash Management* (現金管理暫

行條例) and was drafted by the Central Bank's General Planning Department in which I worked at the time. I had attended many discussions and voiced my doubts about the usefulness of the regulation. Anti-money laundering was a concept the central bank officials had not heard of. Barely four weeks after the announcement, I wrote for the central bank-run *Journal of Financial Research* (金融研究) under a provocative title, "Is Cash Management Really Necessary?" to question the wisdom of the regulation. The editors at the central bank did not see my article challenging the new law as extraordinary, nor did my direct bosses at the central bank feel particularly upset. Laws are laws, and discussions are discussions. That was and still is the protocol in the government.

Dr. Xie Ping sitting in the cubicle next to me at the central bank was more vocal on a wide range of policies. He became a department head of the central bank, and then moved on to head the all-powerful Huijin Investment Corporation, the controlling shareholder of major Chinese banks on behalf of the government. Neither Xie nor I was punished for being outspoken and critical. Four months after I published that critical article, I received a rare and prestigious scholarship from the government to pursue a higher degree at the Australian National University.

Western observers often mistake senior Chinese officials' views or public statements as the official positions. They find it strange that even senior officials openly disagree with their direct bosses. There are no spokesmen in most Chinese government departments or entities. It is confusing to the outsiders that a large number of officials publicly make conflicting statements. But that cacophony is the norm.

They Love the State Sector, Honestly

Having just recently come out of a Socialist planned economy, the Chinese are still grappling with the ideology drilled into their brains since 1949. To the vast majority of Chinese, the centrally-planned economic system until the 1990s still has profound influence. While the central government's comprehensive plans down to such details as the number of toothbrushes the country should produce in each of the next five years (as they planned in the 1950s to 1970s) sound a bit absurd these days, the public still wants the government to plan big items, such as power generation capacity, highways, ports and roads, investments, and utilities prices. Amid information overload, the official Five-Year Plans are still the most important documents analysts and observers pore over and glean for clues.

When I started my career at the central bank in Beijing in 1986, the civil service of the state sector was still the dominant employer. In the following two decades, however, civil service and the SOEs gradually lost their shine and the brightest graduates either chose to go to the West to pursue further education or join the booming private sector, including working for multinational companies operating in China. In the past six or seven years, however, the tide has largely reversed.

Each year since 2006, millions of university graduates have had to fight for a limited number of job vacancies in the civil service through the entrance exams. Their success ratio is very low: 50 or 100 applicants to one vacancy, for example. Compensation in the civil service is low, but higher than most parts of the private sector. Most importantly, it offers employees stability and security.

//Each year, millions of university graduates scramble for a small number of civil service jobs. It is a depressing scene. But it tells you what the public thinks of the state.//

Many commentators attribute the mass rush into civil service in China to the applicants' expectation to take bribes in the future. That is a ludicrous accusation. While corruption is indeed rampant, using that factor to explain a powerful phenomenon is far-fetched in my opinion.

Ha-Joon Chang of Cambridge University described a strange phenomenon in South Korea where an extraordinarily high proportion of students wanted to enter medical schools in the past decade precisely because, after the Asian Financial Crisis in 1997 to 1998, the Korean government drastically cut the welfare state, and job security in the country was further reduced. Many who lost their jobs mid-career end up having to lower their standards of living sharply as they join the permanently unemployed. In comparison, medical doctors at least can opt to open their own clinics if they were to lose their jobs, and they can choose to work for as long as they like, rather than accept dwindling pensions after their mandatory retirement age.

This story is now replayed in China, though it is replayed in the civil service. Civil servants (and to some extent, state sector jobs) still enjoy the highest job security, and are respected in society (contrary to Western perception, again). Equally important, their retirement benefits are significantly more assured than in the private sector.

After a golden period of about 15 years (1992–2007), China's private sector has lost much of its attractiveness as the number of bankruptcies surged and the outlook darkened.

Some commentators have argued that the rush to civil service is irrational, since entry-level civil servants have to work 10 to 20 years to just cover their education expenses — assuming that they do not spend their salaries at all. Whatever the correct calculation may be, human behavior is not always rational. In China, as well as in South Korea, the public is effectively calling for a bigger welfare state, and more job security. The misallocation of human resources in society proves that a smaller government (or a smaller state sector) is not in the best interests of the country.

Central Planners are Here to Stay

The central planners, particularly those sitting in the National

Development and Reform Commission (NDRC), are still by far the most dominant bureaucrats in the Chinese government. While some liberal commentators call for the downsizing and even the abolition of the NDRC, no one seriously thinks that is possible in the foreseeable future. The NDRC, together with many other government departments (at five layers of the government), regulate almost every aspect of business.

To get anything done, even as a small businessman, you must get endorsement from numerous bureaucrats. Ha-Joon Chang talked about his native country, South Korea. In the early 1990s, a Hong Kong-based magazine, *Far Eastern Economic Review*, reported that, to open up a factory in South Korea, you had to obtain 299 permits from 199 agencies. In China, I feel it is pretty similar today — though you may not need 299 permits. Given the cobweb of regulations, imagine how much resistance there is if the top politicians suddenly decided that most regulations must be dismantled because they are bad for the country! Imagine also how difficult and complex it would be. Every now and then, the Chinese government would announce the abolition of a large number of rules and regulations, but new rules and regulations would also be invented to fill their void. So the business sector always finds it hard to breathe. Indeed, as it is costly to learn new rules all the time, some businessmen jokingly begged for the government to keep the status quo: "At least we know the route of getting these permits under the current regime. If you change the rules, we have to re-learn the tricks."

In early 2013, I wrote a blog post in China, complaining about the two months it took me to set up a small advisory company in Guangzhou alongside the microcredit company I was managing. Some commentators half-jokingly said that it took me a shorter time because I was a "celebrity" who often criticized the government.

All said, for China to embrace free market theories, at least two decades must pass. In other words, those born in the 1960s and 1970s who have been intoxicated by central planning must fade into the background. Even after that, there is no guarantee that a truly free market reform will become a reality.

The Satisfaction of Working for SOEs

It is probably a syndrome of thinking of "greener pastures." Many employees at SOEs moan about bureaucracy, inefficiency, and corruption. Many in the private sector complain about their harsh and selfish bosses, and the lack of trust and due process.

One thing seems to come out consistently from my interviews with employees from both sides of the aisle: Employees in the private sector think they work for their bosses and do not have much say in decision-making, while SOE employees have a stronger sense of being their own masters. In the past seven decades, the Communist Party has nurtured the idea of "workers being their own masters" backed up by lifetime employment. At Shenzhen Investment, for example, I was able to criticize the chairman and CEO harshly at a public forum for failing to sack Lin Minrui. What I did was not exceptional at the state sector. For decades, the government has encouraged it. I was but a product of that era. Today, the relatively equal status of employees at SOEs remains intact. That is a very significant factor in the well-being of the workforce. Sadly, that is lacking in the private sector.

It is risky to generalize but the state sector remains the most attractive place to work for most Chinese, according to numerous placement officers at Chinese universities. Apart from the millions of graduates that compete for a small number of civil service jobs in the annual entrance exams, the private sector finds it hard to lure SOE employees away.

The stability of jobs in the state sector has for decades created a sense of belonging and of community. My parents-in-law used to work for Nanjing Petrochemical, an SOE under Sinopec. They retired at the customary age of 60 two decades ago. Today, they still receive 3,000 yuan each per month, a small sum, but they get by with this plus their savings. They get to keep their small flat in Nanjing (in a staff compound where every family used to work or still works at Nanjing Petrochemical). Eleven years ago, they moved to Shanghai, but they are invited back each year for the staff reunion by the trade union of Nanjing Petrochemical, and once every few years, there is a group tour for all the retirees when former colleagues catch up, renew friendships, and swap gossip. While this is happening in some better-established private sector firms, the private sector as a whole is still too young to build this type of soft infrastructure. So far, the private-sector employment is still characterized by many short-term stints, sweatshops, and an inner core of trusted employees around the controlling shareholders. Given the short history of private sector capitalism, there is no public company with diverse shareholding similar to IBM or Qualcom. The most common private-sector business in China is controlled by one family (usually the first-generation entrepreneurs) surrounded by a few relatives and trusted insiders.

First-Generation Entrepreneurs and Mistrust

In the private sector, due to systematic discrimination, poor access to credit, diseconomies of scale, and mismanagement, a large number of businesses behave like flashes in the pan. Tens of thousands go bankrupt or choose to wrap up operations each year, and most do not survive beyond a decade. That takes a toll on the workforce. As a result, these companies cannot afford to plan for the long term, and they do not have the willingness and resources to train their workforce. It becomes a vicious cycle.

In contrast, at Shenzhen International where I served as a director, the company set up an in-house Executive MBA Program several years ago. Due to higher wages, on-the-job training, and the scope for the staff to have an input in the business, staff turnover is extremely low.

PARTY MAN, COMPANY MAN

At Guangzhou Investment, staff morale is high because the company goes from strength to strength. In 2013, the group company acquired the control of a Hong Kong-listed bank, turned around its domestic broker-dealer, built a microcredit company, and disposed of some underperforming units. In fact, all the four listed companies in Yuexiu Group have improved their performance considerably in recent years.

It is true that most private-sector firms are more nimble and more efficient than SOEs, but when they grow, they suffer from a lack of institution and governance structure. Most key shareholders complain that they cannot afford to take a holiday, as everything has to go through them — the only boss — and it slows things down. One private-sector real estate developer insists on approving all architectural designs of all his company's projects and the finished products before launching a pre-sale. In 2011, when his company expanded into 25 cities across China, he could not cope and so bought a personal jet. But still there is a bandwidth problem, and the boss himself has become the bottleneck of the whole business.

In some private businesses, tax evasion, multiple sets of accounts, outrageous entertainment expenses, dubious payments, and reluctance to use IT infrastructure also force the boss to tightly control everything. It also means that they will do everything possible to prevent a sale of their business as a sale would expose everything, including problematic dealings of the past many years. In the past decade, I have participated in a few merger and acquisition deals and initially I did not understand why the entrepreneur would refuse an apparently attractive deal. But when this becomes a pattern, I started to understand why. I reflected on the saga of Enron or Olympus: would the management block an insanely attractive takeover bid just because of their special purposes vehicles or hidden losses that had been covered up for many years?

I have seen the chairman of a 4 billion U.S. dollar Chinese

company (market value) sign for the reimbursement of travel expenses. His business grows fast, and he remains hands-on in the business as he has built it from scratch. In 2012 I formed a joint venture investment company with him. After I discovered a private equity investment opportunity, he wanted to see it first. Fair enough. But his schedule was so tight that he could only see it three weeks later. I eventually chose to unwind that joint venture.

Those above-mentioned strange things are impossible to imagine in Shenzhen Investment, and the other two SOEs I served in. Some SOEs evade taxes and have secret slush funds, but the extent of the problems is much smaller, and by and large there are checks and balances. They behave more like a public company you see in the United States.

13
Chapter

**Answering Critics:
Case Studies, Facts,
and Figures from
China's State Sector**

In this chapter I will first provide three case studies on how and why China's SOEs have outperformed their private sector rivals. Two common themes should become clear. First, SOEs benefit unfairly from systematic advantages over their private sector rivals. Second, SOEs are improving their games under pressure from the public and the government.

Note that these three companies happen to be middle-of-the-roaders, and are probably representative of the wider state sector. I ran the first, and sat on the boards of directors of the other two from 2006 to 2008.

Shenzhen Investment: In eight years, Shenzhen Investment saw its sales surge from just 2 billion to 8.7 billion yuan. The last column in the table shows that the compound growth rates of sales, net profits, and total assets in the eight-year period have — generally — been above 20%, which is high by anyone's standards.

After Hu and Zhang retired in 2009, Guo Liming (former head of SASAC in the Shenzhen City Government) became chairman and CEO for an unremarkable three-year stint. He was followed by Lu Hua who's been at the helm since 2013. The company remains privileged due to its excellent access to bank credit. Note that its bank credit has grown at a compound annual rate of 21% in the past eight years.

Shenzhen International: Shenzhen International is better managed than Shenzhen Investment as it has reported higher growth rates in sales and earnings in those eight years. Sadly, its toll road division was brought down by one giant disaster (Jingnian Expressway). In the second half of 2013, Jingnian Expressway started to record 40% plus traffic growth from a low base. There is finally light at the end of the tunnel.

Guangzhou Investment: Guangzhou Investment's results are similar to those of the other two companies: consistent performance underpinned by good access to cheap credit. Its parent company took control of a listed bank in Hong Kong in 2013. The group has grand ambitions in empire building.

Compound annual growth rate (CAGR) of three companies, 2004–2012

	2004	2007	2008	2010	2012	CAGR
Shenzhen Investment Limited (0604 HK)						
Sales (million CNY)	2,022	3,428	4,208	6,566	8,661	19.9
Net profit (million CNY)	423	1,715	873	1,325	2,156	22.6
Total Asset (million CNY)	11,332	25,526	27,719	33,818	54,392	21.7
ROE (%)	10.02	21.05	8.50	10.24	13.03	—
Total bank loans (million CNY)	4,872	9,638	12,251	12,498	22,210	20.9
Shenzhen International Holdings Limited (0152 HK)						
Sales (million CNY)	272	4,745	5,303	4,385	4,688	42.7
Net profit (million CNY)	335	1,988	507	1,089	1,523	20.8
Total Asset (million CNY)	3,638	21,929	23,736	31,311	34,366	32.4
ROE (%)	12.65	37.60	9.49	14.32	15.74	—
Total bank loans (million CNY)	128	8,807	10,857	11,870	14,571	80.7
Guangzhou Investment (Yuexiu) (0123 HK)						
Sales (million CNY)	4,834	4,911	2,785	5,634	8,120	6.7
Net profit (million CNY)	290	966	536	919	2,482	30.8
Total Asset (million CNY)	26,030	41,274	37,862	50,781	69,997	13.2
ROE (%)	4.66	8.58	4.30	6.76	11.69	—
Total bank loans (million CNY)	6,473	11,823	8,943	17,736	20,131	15.2

Source: The companies' annual reports.

What I Learned from the Three Companies

Modern corporate governance is still a relatively new concept. But slowly and steadily, the concept is taking root in China's state sector. Checks and balances are being introduced. Outside (and independent) directors have been hired and given the necessary respect. In many cases, these outside directors have started to exercise their rights vigorously. Even in Europe and the U.S., the boards of directors often fail to prevent abuse and fraud, and therefore one must be patient in waiting for checks and balances in China to take effect. But I am encouraged by the widespread phenomenon in China that institutional structures are being put in place for modern corporate governance.

> **//SOEs are adapting to public pressure for efficiency and transparency. //**

While fraud and corruption are rampant in China's state sector, there are efforts by the government to minimize the damage. Offenders are being punished and loopholes plugged. In the three state-controlled companies, quite a few senior executives have been brought to justice. Despite known damage to efficiency, the auctions and tender system has been introduced when a state-controlled business makes a significant purchase. Over time, the system will take root, and will get improved to minimize losses in efficiency.

While cronyism, favoritism, and nepotism are endemic, the government and the public both see these things as necessary if a company is to implement a merit-based hiring system and promote employees. I have seen that the selection of senior executives has become more merit-based. The caliber of the senior managers at the three companies has been improving over time. Moreover, the executives are under pressure to learn on the job.

The Sharpest Critic of China's State Sector

Guess who is the sharpest critic of China's state sector? Is it the libertarian economists at Beijing University, the media, or the West? No, you're wrong if you guessed any of them.

It is the Chinese government.

Politicians in the West, for fear of playing into the hands of opposition parties, cannot afford to criticize themselves. But Chinese politicians have the luxury of not having to worry about the opposition, and they are therefore generally more candid. Examples include former Premier Wen Jiabao blasting the Chinese economy publicly and repeatedly for being imbalanced, unstable, and unsustainable. There was also his predecessor, Zhu Rongji, who described the state sector as inefficient and wasteful. Now there is Zhang Yi, the Head of the Chinese Central Government's State-Owned Assets Supervision and Administration Commission (SASAC), who says that the state sector is poorly motivated and in need of revitalization. He vowed to either introduce or expand the mixed economy so as to get rid of the private sector economy vs. state sector economy once and for all.

What debate?

Zhang Yi's predecessors have long defended the financial performance of the state sector while acknowledging the existence of "grave issues" in the state sector. What are those issues?

Foreigners can be forgiven for not understanding the jargon. Let me try and shed a little light.

(1) *Yigududa* (一股獨大) means that the percentage shares held by the government are too big. Many officials and members of the public blame the ills of the state sector on *yigududa*. I never understood their logic. If 100% ownership by the government is too much, at many SOEs where the government controls as little as 20%, none of the "grave issues" — corruption and inefficiency — have gone away. As long as the government still calls the shots, it does not matter if its stake is 100%, 52%, or even 10%.

(2) A mixed economy. Many officials and observers have proposed public-private partnerships, taking their cue from

the same concept that has gained currency in the West in recent years. But this concept contains the same flaws as *yigududa* as we discussed above. Thousands of companies listed on the stock exchange already have "mixed ownership." But the government is too dominant and the private sector shareholders can only be passive and inconsequential. Yes. You are a shareholder, but the government never discusses with you the removal and appointment of the management of, say, China Mobile, the Bank of China, or Yanzhou Coal.

(3) *Guquan fenzhi* (股權分置). This term is impossible to translate into English. I tried but failed. What it means is that the government must compensate the minority shareholders if its majority stake were to be allowed to be traded. Since 1992, over 2000 SOEs went public on the stock exchanges of Shanghai and Shenzhen. But the government's controlling shares were not allowed to be traded. Many officials and members of the public believed that this state of affairs (*yigududa*) had caused the stock market to perform poorly. So they must be allowed to trade. But to allow them to trade, the controlling shareholder (the state) must compensate the long-suffering minority shareholders. In 2005 to 2007, the government forced itself to do this, and the consequence was a total disregard of rules and contracts. After the minority investors received the compensation, the stock market continued to go south.

(4) A system of annual wages (年薪制). Chinese wages are usually paid each month, but in recent years there has been a lot of hot air about introducing a system of annual wages for executives. But is the annual wage not 12 times the monthly wage? No, apparently not. What the proponents of this idea are proposing is giving executives a lump sum base salary for the year (still paid monthly), and then a bonus. Why not just say it clearly and simply?

But the government and Chinese critics have got the issue wrong. *Yigududa* is not an issue at all. They complain that the government's percentage shares are too big. But what's wrong with that?

Whether it has 100%, or 20%, as long as the government remains the controlling shareholder, it will still call the shots. In many companies like Chong Kong or other listed companies, the controlling shareholders only hold 20% to 40%. But they are still the boss, because other shareholders are too diverse and small.

Be Careful What You Wish For

When it comes to the debate of state capitalism vs. private sector capitalism, observers tend to have overly strong views and quickly divide into two distinct camps: most people in the West choose to be free-market libertarian and a minority are left to be interventionist Keynesian, with very few in the middle.

I must say that, having worked in both sectors, I am a middle-of-the-roader and have no strong ideological inclination. But if there is one thing that I want the readers of this book to take away, it is that, in my opinion, both the state sector and pure private sector capitalism have considerable flaws, and that, given China's historical and cultural background, the Chinese have chosen the state sector. If a referendum were to take place today on that issue, I suspect that the Chinese people would favor the status quo. It is a choice thing. We may or may not like it, but we should understand it, and respect it.

[For an insider's critique of China's state sector, please see the appendix.]

I'd like to examine the serious consequences of the retreat by the state from the rural economy. While I will use my hometown in central Hubei Province as an example, it is the same across the country.

Between the early 1950s and early 1980s, the Chinese countryside was organized into Communist communes where every peasant farmer worked like workers and did not pay much attention to the productivity or the outcome of their work. I myself worked in the field while a high school student in 1970 to earn "work points" — a kind of unit of accounting to reflect the time and efforts you put in during a given day. Out of a maximum of 10 points each day, my parents would normally earn 9 or 9.5 points, and I would earn 7 to 8 points. At the end of each year, the village head, accountants, and the Communist Party boss would announce how much, in terms of yuan, each "work point" was worth. That's the take-home net profit in cash. For example, in 1978, my village's work point was worth 0.1 yuan, while the neighboring village's was worth 0.2 yuan. That meant that they were more productive and wealthier. So my parents took home only 720 yuan for the whole family's efforts for the full year 1978.

The biggest problem with a Communist commune was that there were no motivation and incentives to do things better and smarter. That has caused starvation in many parts of China, and poverty across the country. My village was fortunate enough never to have to suffer starvation but as a kid I saw some beggars coming from Henan Province in the north. After the famine in many parts of China, including Henan Province, coupled with the construction of the Danjiankou Reservoir bordering Henan and Hubei provinces in 1968, the government moved 49,000 rural residents from Xichuan County of Henan Province to settle in a big village, Dachaihu, not far away from my village. (Today, the population in Dachaihu has more than doubled to 105,000.) Since 1968, there has been no major communal clash between Dachaihu and the neighboring villages despite their taking large chunks of our land and having very different dialects and customs. In India, Pakistan, Bangladesh, the Philippines, Thailand, and many parts of Africa, and Latin America, communal violence is a depressing phenomenon. But I never heard of such a thing growing up in rural China, despite there being critical disputes over land

and water. When 49,000 people with major cultural differences suddenly migrated to my neighboring region in 1968 and took away large tracks of land, there had been no communal disputes, let alone violence. Clearly grassroots governments have done a brilliant job of steadying things and ensuring social harmony.

Some critics would argue that this was due to the homogenous nature of the Chinese race. In fact, there is no such thing as the Chinese race. Like India, China is a country full of a very diverse people. China's history of 5,000 years is one of frequent wars, fights, and sectarian violence. China was never one country until relatively recently. Indeed, the Qing Dynasty never unified the whole of China. In thousands of years, independent states were formed and disintegrated, and boundaries redrawn again and again, just like in India.

But how did China root out communal violence? By building intricate networks where state institutions were linked all the way down to the village levels and much further. Below the central government, there are provinces, prefectures, counties, towns, villages, and brigades (or groups). So, there are seven layers of government and at each of these seven layers, there are well-paid officials and well-funded institutions to ensure the rule of law.

As someone who grew up in that environment, I know my fellow citizens have complaints about some loss of liberty and the costs to the taxpayer, but we have gained safety, security, and assurance. That's vitally important to the functioning of a normal society.

Contrary to Western critics who argue that the networks are designed to control and rule the people, these institutions are constructive and helpful in defusing violence, and resolving disputes. There is nothing wrong in maintaining control and rule: it is the very responsibility of the state.

Since the 1980s, the lowest two of the seven layers of government have been weakened beyond recognition, causing painful adjustments. Many rural victims despair. The exodus into cities and the rising suicide rates are related to the sudden loss of assurance. During a recent trip home, I was shocked to see my brother who was still in the bush tying a military knife under his belt. Asked why he bothered to do this, my brother replied, "It is not as safe here as before."

In my memory, my village was beautiful, roads clean, village halls neat, river flowing, ponds full, and cattle taken care of in the 1960s to 1980s. Apart from the political cleansing and retribution for those who were associated with the Nationalist Party (that had fled to Taiwan in 1949 after losing the civil war to the Communists) and who were landlords during the previous political regime, my village was very close to what you might think was a utopia: clean, simple, austere, egalitarian, self-sufficient, and environmentally friendly. I would say that it was a sustainable way of life, except that we were poor. But again, utopian idealism is never about seeking materialistic gratification.

Sadly, with the dismemberment of the Communist commune, and the distribution of land to individual families, all infrastructure was quickly destroyed, looted, or run down beyond repair.

In my recent visits to my old village Gongchang, I was very depressed. The small river and ponds had become dry. The roads were no longer usable as they had not been maintained for probably a decade. There was no longer common finance for the village of more than 60 families. And the village halls had been torn down and there was only dust and broken tiles all around. The square where I had learned to ride a bicycle was replaced by two shabby makeshift houses for two elderly couples (one of them was for my uncle and aunt) after their grown-up children had kicked them out.

My uncle hung himself five years ago after his wife died of illness two years earlier. In China, the suicide rate has jumped 60% in the 50 years from 1961 to 2011, according to the official Chinese Center for Disease Control and Prevention. And the rates in the countryside were three times as high as the rates in the cities. The dismantling of the rural quasi-government institutions in the 1980s played a major role in this jump. My uncle's fate was typical for that time.

My parents' next-door neighbors were a couple of blind people. In the Communist Commune system, they were classified as "Wubaohu" (五保户) which meant that they were unable to earn a living, and that the village must provide for their five basic needs: food, clothing, medical care, cash allowances, and political rights. While the assistance was a small sum, it was better than nothing. But in the mid-1980s, when the village government was dismantled, village heads and other mandarins had to go and look for other ways to make a living, and some went to Shenzhen or Shanghai to work in factories. Those who stayed in the village were too busy to mind their own business. After all, they no longer had the mandate and means to do what they used to do (organizing things for all the villagers).

In many parts of China, according to the media and the government, villages had become anarchic institutions. In some places, the elections of village heads had become rigged and corrupt, and even linked to underworld forces. The retreat of the state had left a dangerous power vacuum, and many villagers were left to fend for themselves. Communal violence, rare in the Communist Commune era, was now appearing, similar to what you see in Bangladesh or India. That has reinforced the exodus to the cities.

In my village, the farm field now looks quite barren: one narrow strip of land may be well taken care of, and is growing crops, but the next strip is left growing weeds, because the family that owns the land (strictly speaking, they lease the land for three decades) has long ago migrated to, say, Guangdong, or has chosen not to grow anything at all. That has made it impossible for the remaining villagers to use tractors or common irrigation, and, as a result, farm productivity is declining.

PARTY MAN, COMPANY MAN

Family disputes were previously part of the business of village heads who would mediate and educate all parties to maintain a cordial relationship. If a couple wanted a divorce (which was rare), or if there was domestic violence, village heads would help organize a solution. At SOEs, such as Shenzhen Investment where I served, rules and established ways of doing things were also clear. There was a certain expectation of an employee's behavior at home, at work, and after work. Even today, 35 years after China embarked on economic liberalization, an employee's personal life is not entirely personal. That is one reason why SOEs maintain a kind of family atmosphere. That atmosphere is not without support in the country.

Company heads and particularly heads of local government are expected to behave like "parents (父母官)." In fact, that is exactly what they are called, even today. Many big SOEs (including the three I served) are still organized like a mini-state within a state. For example, in many corporate compounds and community centers, there are post offices, police stations, and catering and education facilities. The heads of the SOEs perform similarly to government officials. They are called the "legs of the government (政府的腿)."

In the cities, there is a grassroots government (to be precise, it is a quasi-government similar to village heads in the bush) called a "neighborhood residents' committee" in each small district. Whatever libertarian critics say about these committees, they have made contributions to family planning, the local environment, moral standards, and crime prevention. The fading role of these committees in recent decades has caused rising crime and a diminishing sense of community in many cities. Now the citizens are calling for a strengthened role for them.

Since March 2013, President Xi Jinping advocated a self-criticism movement within the government. It received ridicule from the West. Even some members of the Chinese public were skeptical. But there are enough true believers in that mechanism.

In fact, it has been a long tradition in China, not so much for the Communist Party as for the governing class in general. At the three SOEs I served, we regularly held meetings to reflect on what we have done and how we have done things. They are not dissimilar to the post-mortems I participated in after losing a major investment banking deal while at UBS, or the semi-annual performance measurement meetings (PMM).

Is China "State Capitalist" or Still Communist?

In the past six to seven decades, the wars and cold wars between the capitalist West and Communist blocs have persisted. With the disintegration of the Soviet Union some two decades ago, and the transformation of China, there are just a few remaining ideologically Communist states in the world. To me, China has transformed itself probably too fast, though it has probably handled the transformation better than the Soviet Union. In both countries, however, the transformation has caused massive inequality and social discontent. The lesson there is to engineer a gradual change for the public to adapt. The way I see it, China has gone backward in the past decade (see the statistics in Chapter 11). This reversal is pragmatic, and maybe even needed.

Just one year before I joined Shenzhen Investment, the city government even flirted with the idea of selling its entire stake in the listed company to an entrepreneur for as little as 1 billion yuan, to be paid in three installments. The decision was put on hold only due to fear of job losses. I learned this only after I came aboard. Even when I was at Shenzhen Investment, the entrepreneur had lobbied the city government to re-consider the sale. But today, the state's stake is worth more than 10 billion yuan, and the labor force has doubled. In the meantime, the other two SOEs I served as a director of, Shenzhen International and Guangzhou Investment, have also seen their market value rise manifold. This has created substantial value for the tax-payer, and it has created jobs.

A Soviet-style "shock therapy"

Many observers (including some economists at Beijing University) argue that China's state sector and the overall governance of the country are so rotten that only a sort of "shock therapy" will get the country out of misery. But the experience following the collapse of the Soviet Union was not encouraging. In China, if Soviet-style "shock therapy" were to be performed, I can guess that only the elites would grab assets and power, and that would worsen inequality and even lead to social unrest.

In December 2013, the central government released its audit of all local government debts. It came out to be 18 trillion yuan as of June 2013, equivalent to 30% of GDP, compared to 25% of GDP three years ago. These figures seem manageable in comparison to some in Japan, some European countries, and the U.S., but its growth rate is worrying: it was up 70% from three years ago.

Solution? The National Development and Reform Commission (NDRC) immediately assured the market not to worry: some local governments will be allowed to roll over the debts, in other words, they will be allowed to borrow more. That is of course the classic way of kicking the can down the road. Given the impact of shadow banking, and the increase of market interest rates, it is a safe bet that the local governments will have to pay more to roll over their debts. Given the weak cash flows of many local governments, it is conceivable that they will have to sell businesses, including many utilities, the controlling stakes in banks, insurers, real estate holdings, and industrial companies.

It is possible that the governments of Shenzhen and Guangzhou will have to sell their controlling stakes of the three SOEs I served. But given continued good performance of these and many similar SOEs, taxpayers will get good deals when the inevitable arrives.

Gauging the populist trend

It is interesting to gauge what the public wants from what the politicians do. For example, kissing babies, visiting the elderly, and kicking footballs are universally conducive in winning the hearts and minds of the public. In some countries, selling state assets is seen as popular. For example, British politicians like to make a point about their vows to sell government stakes in RBS and Lloyd's Bank, having done well in the flotation of Royal Mail in late 2013. In the U.S., politicians like to beat the drum about exiting not only quantitative easing, but also exiting government stakes in Citigroup and GM. To me, that suggests that politicians think that the public wants free capitalism, or freer capitalism.

In China, while politicians do not have to buy votes, the pressure to be popular and gain respect remains important. Listen to what they say and look at what they do. They talk about the "critical role for the state sector, and a supplementary role for the private sector." Apart from their action that has led to almost the full-scale reversal of the economic liberalization of the previous two decades, the government is trying to win the hearts and minds of the public by sharply expanding the state sector via infrastructure programs.

Private sector banks

Banking has long been considered the province of the state. Of the thousands of banks of all shapes and forms in China today, the biggest and arguably the only private sector player is Minsheng Bank which accounts for a mere 3% of the sector's total deposits, while the big five banks account for about 60%.

The Communist Party Third Plenum proclaimed that the private sector would be allowed to set up banks. Big deal! The media made lots of noise about it. But I urge caution. The reality is that this sort of rhetoric is not new, and it will be many years before rhetoric becomes action. Even if the government were to slam the door open to the private sector banks, there would be a whimper not a bang. And why? China is already hugely over-banked, and better-quality customers are already in the folds of the existing banks, and the banking business is sticky.

In other words, high quality customers are unlikely to switch away from the state banks.

Indeed, in this over-banked market, the existing banks have already dipped into the subprime lending business on the back of competitive pressure and surplus lending capacity. New entrants will face an uphill battle to attract good-quality customers on the one hand, and on the other hand, will have to take unnecessary risks in the leftover subprime segment. After all, some Chinese banks have become so big and so well-entrenched that any new entrants will be minuscule and weak.

Who is Moving the Chinese Banks' Cheese?

Within just five months, Yuebao, the e-finance partnership between China's Alibaba, and a fund house, Tianhong, raised 250 billion yuan from millions of little guys to invest in money market funds and treasury bonds. Other Internet companies such as Tencent and Sina.com are also launching similar services.

All of a sudden, the market is euphoric about the beginning of the end of China's stodgy and bureaucratic banks. After all, these banks are predominantly state-controlled and have never been nice to the little guys. That a sleek new force is coming out of nowhere to challenge the bloated and entrenched banks is an exciting development.

Except that the story is just a story. The reality is that it is not easy to move the cheese of the Chinese banks. Not yet, at least. Let's look at some inconvenient truths.

First of all, despite the hoopla, the 250 billion yuan is just 0.2% of the banking sector's total deposit base.

Second, none of these e-commerce companies and e-finance platforms has an established base of borrowers or banking skills. Moreover, they do not even have lending licenses. Strictly speaking, the buying and selling of money market funds by Yuebao may be considered a violation of regulatory rules. It is a clever innovation, and the regulators have so far turned a sympathetic eye to this borderline case. But if it spreads like wildfire, the regulatory sympathy could evaporate.

Third, how are Alipay or other similar operators going to use the money they raise from the little guys? So far, their only options are money market funds, treasury bonds, and bank deposits. But money market funds must in turn invest the money somewhere, predominantly in bank deposits and treasury bonds. So, in a way, instead of competing with the banks, the likes of Yuebao are working for the banks. Of course, the maneuver by the likes of Yuebao will raise the returns for the millions of little guys, but those returns will be capped by the willingness of the banks to accept the recycled money. It is true that the work of Yuebao and its rivals will push up the cost of funding for the whole banking industry, but the extent of that funding cost increase is totally dependent on the banks' ability to pass the higher funding costs to borrowers. At present, there is a significant scope for the banks to increase lending rates, judging from huge amounts of unmet demand for credit.

On the face of it, the little guys are moving money from bank deposits to buy financial products. But given the size of the banking industry in China, the banks collectively determine the yields and prices of financial assets.

Finally, one must ask the question why Google and Amazon, for all their resources and popularity, do not do what Yuebao is doing. The reason is simple: the business model does not exist in the United States. Why? Because of the free market interest rate regime. But as much as a quarter of the funding for China's banks is already driven by market interest rates. That is the so-called wealth management products. In this particular segment, the banks actually make higher interest margins because they more than just pass the higher funding costs to the end-users of the money. They charge multiple service fees as well as charging higher interest rates.

It is conceivable that if, in the next five to 10 years, all the funding sources of the banks will be subject to market rates, thanks to the pressure from the likes of Yuebao. The banks' lending rates will move up in a parallel manner, with banks' profitability either unchanged or even enhanced. As we approach that stage, Yuebao and the like will gradually lose their relevance. By then, they either become glorious martyrs for the Chinese banking liberalization, or invent something else.

At present, Yuebao and the like are harmless to the banks. When they start to move the banks' cheese, the banks will fight back by simply raising interest rates, one way or another, to keep deposits, eliminating the scope for the recycling of deposits. The likes of Yuebao will still have their usefulness: pooling the money of the little guys to invest in treasury bonds and money market funds. But that business model has no "moat": the banks can do this for the millions of their customers at tiny marginal cost. Thus far, they have not bothered to do it. But if the need arises, who is there to stop the banks from offering even better products, given their vast capabilities to cross-subsidize between various lines of business?

After all, investing in money market funds and treasury bonds is not risk-free. One wave of losses on the back of some volatility is sufficient to cool the euphoria we have so far witnessed.

In conclusion, the likes of Yuebao are doing Chinese savers a great service. Their continued efforts will force the banks to gradually raise the interest rates on short-term deposits, one way or another, with the rate hike officially sanctioned by the central bank or without. As a result, the yield curve in the banking sector will experience a parallel shift upward. In the long term, that means a slowdown of total credit growth, and a more rational economy. The banks will be able to operate in a healthier environment.

14

Chapter

What's Wrong with China's Private Sector?

PARTY MAN, COMPANY MAN

As a Chinese citizen, I am not sure if I want a bigger state sector or a bigger government. I dread overregulation and stifling rules as much as the next guy. As I detailed in my book *Inside China's Shadow Banking: The Next Subprime Crisis?*, many regulations and rules in China do not make sense. But these rules exist and are very hard to get rid of... even when everyone agrees that they do not make sense. Of course, you will never get everyone to agree on something, or anything. So, we kick the can down the road and try and muddle through for as long as we can.

You, as one of my readers, do not really care about what I think should happen to China's state sector or the government. What realistically will happen is far more important.

I can make a few conclusions in that regard:

1. The state sector is far more dominant in China than most observers think it is.
2. Between 1978 and about 2003 — a total of 25 years — the significance of China's state sector declined as a result of economic liberalization, but the trend has been reversed in the past decade.
3. The state sector may very well grow its dominance over the economy in the next decade because of the deficiency of the private sector, the enormous challenges facing the world economy, and China's own social and economic problems.

I am not just saying these things today because it is fashionable to do so after the ascent of the Keynesian interventionist theory following the U.S. subprime crisis. I have been saying these things all along.

In my October 4, 2005, op-ed for the *Financial Times*, "China's Private Sector in Shadow of the State," I poured cold water on the mainstream view that confused wishful thinking with reality.

I wrote then:

It is fashionable these days to announce [a] claim that China's private sector accounts for half or even two-thirds of the economy but nothing can be further from the truth, in my view. Despite two decades of deregulation and privatization, the private sector still lives in the state's shadow and has limited access to finance and markets. This debate is not academic because it is about the efficiency and sustainability of the world's fastest growing major economy. It is also important to the understanding of China's business cycles.

Let us look at some simple facts. The private sector makes up about 40 of the 1,600 Chinese companies listed on the domestic and overseas bourses and their combined market capitalization is less than 3% of the total. In the banking market, less than 10% of credit goes to private enterprises. Official data shows that the private sector is responsible for less than one-third of gross domestic product. In terms of asset values, the private sector is even smaller. Despite inaccuracies in the official data, I see no reason to reject them in favor of non-government estimates.

Look again at who calls the shots in major business sectors. The state sector controls either the whole or the majority of the following big sectors: oil, petrochemicals, mining, banks, insurance, telecommunications, steel, aluminum, electricity, aviation, airports, railways, ports, highways, automobile manufacturing, healthcare, education, and the civil service.

It is sometimes hard to be precise about the nature of a company's ownership because of its listing status or various joint ventures. However, looking at the league tables of even the four most deregulated sectors suggests to me that the state-owned enterprises remain very significant or even dominant. They include the white goods, retail, textiles, and beverage sectors. In these sectors, the ownership restrictions were lifted as early as the late 1970s, but the private sector is still playing second fiddle.

I continued in the op-ed:

The private sector is still subject to widespread discrimination, although the constitutional amendments of 2002 officially gave the private sector equal rights. Till this day, private sector companies are still not allowed to operate in too many "strategically important sectors" such as banking, insurance, telecoms, railways, ports, oil and petrochemicals. The list is long. Risk-averse bankers also shy away from the private sector.

More than eight years later, the state sector's dominance has not changed much, with some relatively minor exceptions. More private-sector companies have gone public in the stock exchanges but most of them are too small to make a difference to affect the dominance of SOEs. The insurance sector has opened the door a bit wider to foreign players and the private sector, but that was after the state-controlled insurers had become so entrenched and the marginal benefits of investments in the sector had been falling. Not surprisingly, new entrants are all bleeding red ink, and some cannot see light at the end of the tunnel.

In the retail sector, while the door has been completely open to the private sector and foreign operators, it is a fiercely competitive sector and, with the new electronic commerce players, like Alibaba, Taobao, JD, Dangdang, and Suning, the economics look bleaker than ever. And even in this sector, SOEs may still account for a third or even a half of the market share.

What is wrong with China's private sector? In a previous chapter, I highlighted some of its weaknesses, namely, they are still too small, too inexperienced, and financially too weak. Many of them do not have a long-term commitment, and tend to be opportunistic. Why should they not be? The social attitude towards the private sector is not exactly friendly, and the legal system is not robust enough to defend their rights after all. Partly because of their greed and partly because of their short-termism, we have seen many frauds and misdeeds by the private sector, further reinforcing the public prejudice against them, and further playing into the hands of hawkish elements in the government that call for tougher regulations and more involvement of SOEs. In this book, I will not analyze which is cause and which is effect, but will just point to the mutual reinforcement of each other.

Here, I will highlight two related factors for the plight of the private sector: One is the systematic discrimination against the private sector by the government and the public. We analyzed this in the awarding of government contracts (utilities, and construction, and indeed any type of concessions). But the discrimination does not end there. Due to long-standing interest rate controls (below inflation rate), bank credit is a very significant form of subsidy to borrowers. As a banker, you often have the same self-censorship in granting credit as a city mayor in the awarding of a utilities concession or a construction contract. As a lending officer working for a government bank, if you lend to an SOE and the loan eventually goes bust, you may be held responsible, but the penalty will be minor — as long as you did not take bribes and the credit assessment procedure is robust enough. However, if the defaulted loan was owed by a private-sector borrower, you will be in deep trouble — in some cases, even if you have been squeaky clean and the credit assessment has been done properly. You will likely be made subject to a series of unpleasant investigations. If the investigations do not turn up anything fishy, your career may be finished. Or at least your sound sleep may have been destroyed for six months. So as a banker, you will exercise a lot of caution.

PARTY MAN, COMPANY MAN

My younger brother, Hualiang, was head of Golden Shrimp Credit Union in Jingmen City, Hubei Province, until the lender collapsed in 2003. Until this day, the local government's Audit Office still asks him to go and pursue unpaid debtors from time to time. Since about 2000, Chinese banks have phased in a "Life-Time Responsibility System" on lending officers.

Second, as I mentioned in my FT op-ed:

> We need to understand the special circumstances in which the Chinese private sector has grown. Many private entrepreneurs are former officials. Their businesses are also reincarnations of former state-owned enterprises.

Why do I think China will in the next decade expand the role of the state sector and the government? Because of the immense challenges the country faces.

First, the three biggest challenges China faces are resources depletion, environmental damage, and socioeconomic inequality, in my opinion. All these three issues are directly related to population control. In my judgment, that is also the mainstream view in China, although the Western observer may disagree.

Whatever the observers may say about the best way to tackle these three issues, the prevailing view inside China is that a big state sector is consistent with solutions.

For many big environmental and infrastructure projects where direct financial returns are low, there are simply not enough sizable private-sector operators in China. This is due to two factors. First, most Chinese citizens are still too poor to pay for the full price of water, gas, utilities, and infrastructure. Or so they claim. Two, the Communist planned economy continued from 1949 until, well, pretty much recently. The citizenry has been accustomed to not paying at all, or not paying the full price for water, utilities, and infrastructure. Today, for many early-stage sectors and capital-intensive sectors, the state is still the only realistic funder. These types of investments are often high-risk and high-return propositions. The advantages of SOEs are their higher tolerance for risks, much lower funding costs, longer time horizon, and better ability to smooth the losses in one project with profits from other projects.

It is a vicious cycle: the long period of discrimination against the private sector has given rise to a weak private sector. And a weak private sector means that the state must step in constantly. China Development Bank (CDB) controlled by the central government, for example, was charged with the funding of a large number of policy loans in the past few decades (including in its previous life as several entities). The initial mandate for CDB was that it would act as a lender of last resort for risky, and unprofitable long-term infrastructure and industrial projects, often sponsored by other SOEs. But as the economy has grown in the past two decades, the tide has risen. CDB is now one of the most profitable banks in the world.

However, only in hindsight do most of its investments look sensible.

Part of China's way to deal with resource depletion and energy shortages is to seek global supplies. This involves huge investments in other countries. While the private sector has been active, their firepower is limited and their risk appetite is lower. In early December 2013, I spoke at a global mining conference in London. In break-out sessions with a wide range of delegates from all over the globe, there was one common theme of their questions: almost everyone I met with was looking to tap China's outbound investments in the global mining sector, a sector that had been in recession for about two years.

We discussed several ways to link China's money with overseas mining projects.

1. Chinese companies, mostly SOEs (usually the end-

users such as steel mills, aluminum smelters, and copper refiners) directly acquire mines and processing plants in other countries. This has been the main phenomenon in the past two decades.

Unfortunately, they have lost a fortune in the past four or five years as a result of overpaying, mismanagement, bad luck, and resistance from host-countries' political and environmental concerns. While the tide of money flows receded in 2013, there was the perception that they will cease to be the major capital providers in the future. I disagree. This category of investors are more deeply involved in the ebbs and flows of the global mining sector and understand the situation better (or so they claim). I think they will remain the dominant force of investing in overseas mining projects when the next wave of commodity prices increases.

2. Sovereign wealth fund: China Investment Corporation (CIC). To the best of my knowledge, CIC is charged with the responsibility to maximize returns on parts of China's foreign exchange reserves, and it does not have the responsibility to ensure a stable supply of energy and commodities for China. Therefore, its investment in overseas mining projects will always be opportunistic in nature.

3. Private entrepreneurs: I believe they are ill-equipped (more so than SOEs) to navigate the unfamiliar waters involving political, environmental, and social issues of investing in foreign mining projects.

4. Domestic funds (such as Qualified Domestic Institutional Investors [QDII] or private equity funds). In 2007, China approved a few QDII funds for domestic investors to tap the equity market in Hong Kong just in time to suffer the global crash when Lehman Brothers fell. That episode has made domestic investors as well as the government more

timid about overseas financial assets. In my view, it will be many years before Chinese funds become a meaningful force in the global asset market or mining projects.

Enterprising State

In recent years, I have sat on the boards of directors of six private-sector companies, including Fosun (656 HK 復星國際), one of the biggest and most successful private sector businesses. I can see from a different angle how the private sector has to fight on an unlevel playing field.

In 2012, *The Economist* published a special report on "State Capitalism: The Visible Hand." In that report, the state was portrayed as being useful and efficient for some sectors (such as infrastructure) but bad at others (such as consumer goods). But in China's fast-growing consumer sectors, SOEs are adapting to a new reality reasonably well. Many of them are not only surviving but also prospering. For example, a big number of SOE department stores and groceries have gained a new lease on life thanks to the rising throughput and the rising capital value of the premises they have owned.

In the chaotic and scandal-stricken dairy sector, SOEs are dominant, as China Food, Bright Dairy, and Yili play stable roles and—hopefully — they will consolidate the sector and squeeze out the big number of small fly-by-night merchants.

In the highly lucrative traditional liquor sector, there are 50-plus major players from Maotai and Wuliangye to Luzhou Laojiao, and there is no significant presence by the private sector.

In the brewery sector, the dominant three (Tsingtao, Yanjing, and China Resources) have a combined market share of over half. The few second-tier players are also SOEs such as Chongqing and Zhujiang. Foreign companies such as InBev and the Japanese brands are still marginal.

The three Taiwanese food producers (Want Want, Tingyi, and

President) and home-grown Wahaha (drinks and water) dominate the sector of noodles, snacks, and drinking water. Even in this space, SOEs are quite significant.

In the pharmaceutical sector, dominant players are still SOEs, as are medicine distributors and hospitals.

In a book entitled *The Entrepreneurial State*, Mariana Mazzucato challenges the conventional libertarian view that the state's usefulness is just to correct "market failures." She argues that even in the U.S., the so-called free-market champion, the state has consistently, over many decades, played a very significant role in fostering high-tech industries including pharmaceuticals, Internet companies, biotechnology, alternative energy providers, and space programs. Indeed, she argued, that the state has made it possible for some industries to come into being. Mazzucato asserts that the state has been very constructive to the growth of a free market in most countries, including the U.S.

In China, she argued, alternative energy was almost entirely created by the state. I would agree with that. She argues that the state is just as good as the private sector in picking winners. I would go one step further to say that even if the state is unable to pick winners, its presence helps create a market, and steadies it. Having a lower financial return overall is acceptable for the state sector, so long as it creates significant externalities to society at large.

Ugly Merchants

The private sector has a relatively poor image among the Chinese public for a complex set of reasons. That image hinders its growth.

First, the poor image has historical reasons behind it. Between 1949 and probably the 1980s, official propaganda

//The private sector is significantly disadvantaged, politically and culturally.//

has portrayed capitalists as sneaky and ruthless exploiters, and therefore monstrous. It was often said that Communism was paradise and the archenemy of capitalism. Sadly, intense brainwashing is having unpleasant side-effects on the Chinese government and the public even today.

In the 1980s, when China again allowed street hawkers and mom-and-pop shops to exist after having banned them for over three decades, the only people who took up those newly-given "privileges" were four types of people. We can call them "The Old Four Types":

1. Unemployed urbanites, including fresh graduates, and laid-off factory workers;
2. Desperate peasant farmers who had just moved to the city to reunite with their families, including the "Educated Youth" who were sent to the countryside by Chairman Mao in the 1960s and 1970s;
3. Officials who had been sacked for their wrongdoings, and
4. Prisoners who had just been released.

As you can see, these people were the lowest socioeconomic and political classes. To most Chinese who had just come out of the Cultural Revolution, these small-time entrepreneurs were only slightly more respectable than drug addicts and prostitutes.

I have always liked making money and so have struggled with the temptation to make more. I recall vividly how poor my family was in the early 1980s. When I entered the Graduate School of the central bank in Beijing as a cadet, my family and friends were very proud, but still, I could not afford to buy even a much-needed bicycle. Many people envied me for having a bright career ahead of me. But when I saw how street hawkers outside my school campus were selling low quality plastic shoes and sandals, or simply eggs and vegetables and still making 50 yuan a day — equivalent to my monthly salary at the central bank — my pride was severely wounded.

At the time, the compliance rule allowed civil servants to moonlight, for example, by working for private businesses on weekends or in the evenings. But few took up that privilege. Or few would broadcast their moonlighting as it was regarded as low taste and poor form.

Ever a small entrepreneur, I was torn between a respected career at the central bank and making some real money. I quickly found an opportunity in late 1985. My college friend Zhou Xiaoju's father was the sales director at a tractor maker, Shengniu, in Huangshi City, Hubei Province. Tractors were in hot demand and the Chinese factories could not produce them fast enough. However, the retail price of tractors had been fixed for many years and as a result, there was a long queue waiting to buy tractors and a rationing system based on personal relationships became the norm.

I took two weeks off from graduate school and borrowed 10,000 yuan (a huge sum at the time) from a credit union in my hometown on my good standing alone (I had no collateral and collateral was not essential for a loan at the time) and with no single yuan of my own equity. I bought a tractor for that sum of money and hired a driver to drive the 300-kilometer distance to my village. The economy was just in the early stage of a boom, and demand for transport services was extraordinarily high. I had a job at the central bank to go back to. My father was unwilling to learn to drive the tractor so my younger brother, Hualiang, had to take up the driver's job at the tender age of 13. Hualiang was short and small. When he drove the huge tractor towards you, you would think it was a drone coming your way! So, it was dangerous and I decided to sell the tractor.

The price of tractors was higher in the secondhand market than the officially controlled prices for brand new tractors. So I sold my purchase for a 30% mark-up the next week. The net profit of 3,000 yuan was as much as my salary for five years! At the time, there was no requirement for business registration, no sales tax, and no profit tax. While I was thrilled to pocket the windfall gains, it had never occurred to me that I should have quit my job at the central bank and repeat what I had just done, or do what many street hawkers and other business people were busy doing. In fact, I kept my little secret until many years later. Although what I had done was entirely compliant with the rules in the civil service at the time, why would you tell people about making money? It was so low class. In ancient China, there was a way to describe money: "*a du wu* 阿堵物" — "that thing."

In Europe, a change of social attitude toward money and merchants took place slowly in the seventeenth to nineteenth centuries. But sadly, China had to go through that process, yet again, in the 1980s and 1990s after the Cultural Revolution had ended. Today, the Chinese public is much more materialistic than in the past, but their attitude towards other people's pursuit of money is still negative and jealous, if not downright hostile. While the Chinese today are more obsessed with money and making money than people in the West, it is still considered poor form to admit that. For example, China's entrepreneurs still prefer to dress up what they do as "a cause" and "a career pursuit." In 2011 and 2012, when I was still Chairman at Wansui Micro Credit Company in Guangzhou, I lobbied aggressively for the government to remove caps on the industry's financial leverage, and restrictions on our scope of business. One day, I spent an hour discussing with a top regulator in Guangdong Province the benefits of deregulation and the ways to minimize the potential downside risks. At the end of the meeting, the regulator looked mysteriously at me and said: "You are just trying to make more money!"

I almost choked. Speechless for a few long seconds, I shot back, "Yes. I am indeed trying to make more money. But I am a businessman. Is there anything wrong with making more money?"

But I may not be a typical Chinese businessman. A typical

one would skirt that question, and almost apologetically reply: "No, no, no. Making more money is not the issue. I am trying to do what's good for small businesses and customers. This is consistent with the Party's policies. I am just trying to help the whole microcredit sector!"

Each time I attended a conference that had been organized by the microcredit industry, I found speakers talking about grand objectives, such as helping underprivileged customers and upholding ideals of social justice. On January 10, 2012, when I was honored as "A Micro Credit Person of The Year" by the semi-official industry association, I gave a short speech in which I argued that profit-maximization was the ultimate goal of the sector. "If we did not make adequate returns, new money would not flow into the sector, banks would not support us, and our shareholders would pull out. It is just as simple as that!"

I know I made my audience very uncomfortable, particularly those officials who had just given me a medal thanking me for my contributions to the industry.

I find it helpful to admit my real money-making objectives right upfront. When I just joined Shenzhen Investment in 2006, the company's stock surged. There were whispers in the corridors about what I wanted to do. To remove doubt, I made it plain in staff meetings that I was there to make money instead of making friends. That way, I was known as a "Money Man" instead of a "political man." That reputation simplified my life quite a bit. I did not bother to attend some political meetings. It even helped me when I lobbied the city government officials on asset disposals and restructuring.

The first batch of business people (i.e., "The Old Four Types") made a killing for themselves by the mid-1990s. Only then had higher class workers (such as SOE workers, teachers, and even civil servants) started to abandon their dead-end jobs for the private sector. But they were still treated as greedy, and "overly money-minded." I know a lot of cases where families hedged their bets: husbands would dip their toes into the private sector, while their wives must stay firmly in the civil service or an SOE.

In the late 1990s, a large number of poorly performing SOEs were bought or leased by their managers, local bureaucrats, or clever entrepreneurs for a song. They turned these businesses around on the back of picking low hanging fruit: plugging loopholes, repairing leaking pipes, laying off workers, and making the products slightly better. The powerful wave of economic growth in the past two decades has made some of these risk-takers filthy rich by Chinese standards. As a result of the public's envy, and sensational media hype, some of these entrepreneurs have suffered retribution, and others have been caught bribing officials and bankers, short-changing customers, violating environmental regulations, or engaging in unscrupulous consumption. There have been reports every now and then that some of those early deals had not been struck exactly fairly or honestly. For a while, tracing business tycoons' "first pot of gold" became a media sensation: how did they get rich in the first place? The media also loved to report on the spectacular downfalls from grace by high-profile businessmen. While there is a bit of that jealousy in every country and every culture — for example, Lloyd Blankfein, CEO of Goldman Sachs, once remarked that if he were to die suddenly, some people would be pleased — it is probably more so in China today, as many in the public claim that the government has created an unfair environment for all.

Indeed, some Chinese have been more fairly treated than others. There is the institutionalized divide between the urbanites and rural residents. Depressed interest rates on bank deposits and bank loans are nothing short of robbing Paul to subsidize Peter. While liberal economists may argue that the free market and liberalization are the answers to this type of social injustice, the Chinese government and the public call for more forceful intervention by the state.

The Stock Market Made Things Worse

According to the SASAC, a total of 953 state-controlled companies were listed on the two domestic stock exchanges (Shanghai and Shenzhen), accounting for 38.5% of the total number of listed companies as of the end of 2012. But in terms of market value of the listed companies, the state had a market share of 51.4%.

However, these numbers are disputed by independent analysts. According to a search on Baidu.com, the state accounted for about 80% of the market capitalization. That estimate is closer to what I see in the real economy. The reason for this discrepancy is because the government's stakes in some companies have fallen below 50% and have been excluded from the statistics. But the government still calls the shots there.

When China opened its stock market in 1992, the government maintained tight control on who should go public, the IPO stock price, and a host of other parameters. The total number of IPO companies was also controlled. This central control meant several things:

1. SOEs are favored. In the first 14 years (1992 to 2006) of China's experiment with the stock market, those fortunate enough to be given the privilege to go public were normally SOEs, with only a few exceptions. In countless official documents, the stock market was said to be a credit mechanism to "alleviate poverty" for SOEs. At the time, the Party line was this: everyone (even SOEs!) must repay bank credit to ensure the soundness of the banking industry. So we need a stock market to provide permanent capital to impoverished SOEs. This line was widely parroted by politicians and written in government documents and newspapers. Strangely, many in the public who are victim of that theory also subscribe to that theory. Sure enough, most of those lucky companies squandered their new

money. To prevent stock prices from falling too much in light of the IPOs by additional companies, the government had to keep the IPO window narrow enough. That meant that most new IPO companies were still most-favored SOEs. Despite high inflation, the stock-market valuation stayed high, from about 100-times earnings in the 1990s to about 40-times toward 2006.

2. A painful overhang. In the past two decades, the government has tried to achieve two competing objectives in the stock market: raising money to help the struggling state sector, and keep on doing it. But the reality is you cannot fool retail investors all the time. Despite the rapid growth of the economy, the Chinese stock market has continued to de-rate, and public shareholders continue to lose money. To prop up the market, the government tried various tactics such as cutting stamp duties, forcing listed companies to compensate public investors, offering better disclosure, punishing frauds, and suspending new IPOs. As this book is being written (December 2013), new IPOs have been suspended for over one year. This is the fourth time the government has played this trick in the past two decades.

Since 2006, China has allowed a growing number of private-sector companies to go public. The stock exchange even created a section for small and mid-size companies that were mainly from the private sector. In 2012, the government created yet another section, called the Growth Enterprise Market (GEM), to cater to even smaller companies. Because of the huge imbalance between market supply (liquidity) and the small number of companies allowed to go public, this GEM market is characterized by hype, speculation, outrageous valuations, and highly volatile trading. Their price-earnings ratios were often in the range of 60 to 100 times, but sadly many businesses were merely a flash in the pan.

Looking back, China's stock market has been unjustly made

to bail out SOEs at the expense of the public. Since 2006, a big number of small companies have raised money from the stock market, but they pale against the trillions of yuan the SOEs have raised. While the public are proportional shareholders of SOEs such as China Mobile, China Life, or the Bank of China, it is the government that calls the shots, so never be fooled to think the public has a say in how these SOEs are run.

When Entrepreneurs Become Politicians

It happens everywhere in the world, but in China, this is a much more pronounced phenomenon: A big number of entrepreneurs (both established and up-and-coming) want to become part-time politicians. Some are so eager that they even bribe their way into a political career, for recognition, for political protection, and for favors. To be fair, some entrepreneurs become part-time or full-time politicians to make a contribution to society. But the perception is that they are probably in the minority. The voices — increasingly loud voices — by entrepreneurs in the government have added value to the making of laws and policies.

If you look at the five tiers of the government, entrepreneurs occupy a large portion of the parliaments, the executive branches of the government, and the political consultative committees. There is the Industry and Commerce Association (工商聯合會) at every level of the government and they are a semi-official and influential entity.

This flocking of people to politics — without first giving up their own business pursuits, and, indeed, aiming to enhance their own business pursuits — says volumes about the environment in which China's private sector survives. It also reinforces the public perception — no matter how unfair the perception may be — that the private sector is opportunistic, greedy, and selfish. The consequences are far-reaching. The phenomenon, instead of enhancing the private sector's status as an independent and leading force, cements the private sector's position as the second-class force. As the Party likes to say, the private sector is a "supplement" to the state sector (國有經濟的補充).

It is a self-fulfilling process. In the secret liaisons between the government and the entrepreneurs-turned-politicians, deals are struck and favors are granted, and eventually somewhere along the process, the details of the liaisons are leaked, and entrepreneurs humbled. Instead of staying away from politics, more entrepreneurs rush for political protection.

15

Chapter

Unanswered Questions

By now, I hope I have convinced you of the truth of 5 things:

1. The state sector remains the dominant part of the Chinese economy.
2. In the past decade, China has erased most (if not all) of the liberalization of the previous two decades. As a result, the state sector has become more dominant than it was a decade ago.
3. The state sector enjoys widespread public support in China, contrary to perceptions in the West. There are political, social, and cultural reasons for this "strange" situation.
4. The state sector and SOEs are constantly adapting to the public demand for transparency and efficiency. As a whole, they do not necessarily underperform the private sector. Indeed, due to systematic discrimination against the private sector, there is evidence to the contrary: the state sector has had a better financial track record in the past three decades. Indeed, it is not fair to make comparisons given the unleveled playing field.
5. The many challenges China faces today need a robust and well-funded state sector. At least that is, in my judgment, what the Chinese government and most members of the public think. These challenges include social inequality, overpopulation, environmental damage, and the depletion of global resources.

However, there are four major questions I do not have the answers for, but I will provide some preliminary analysis here.

Is the State Sector Crowding In, Or Crowding Out, Private Sector Investments?

The conventional liberal view is that in most cases state-sector investments will crowd out private-sector investments by pushing up the interest rates (and by competing for limited credit resources). Obviously there is a lot of that going on in China today. China's interest rates span a very long spectrum, from under 1% for demand deposits to 3% for 1-year term deposits, 4.5% yield to maturity on 10-year Treasury notes, and 6% 1-year prime lending rates. For the vast majority of private-sector businesses, lending rates range between 10% to 20% and even 30%.

Why such a wide spectrum?

I think the high interest rates small private-sector businesses have to pay is a result of the state sector consuming too much credit, as shown in the examples of the three SOEs I was a Board Director of: Shenzhen Investment, Shenzhen International, and Yuexiu.

The pool of credit resources is always finite, and if SOEs consume more of it, there will be less left for the private sector. Superficially, credit expansion can enlarge the pool of credit, as China has consistently done in the past three decades. But that policy has led to inflation and, consequently, higher nominal interest rates (in the free market, if not in the regulated banking segment). So in real terms, the pool of credit resources remains finite.

On the other hand, many industries and opportunities did not exist until the state stepped in to invest first, such as alternative energy, high speed railroads, ports, expressways, and telecoms. The seemingly irrational investments by the state have created opportunities for the private sector to be subcontractors as well as consumers and partners of those businesses. Some economists call this "crowding in." There is certainly a lot of that in China as well. The issue is whether "crowding out" outweighs "crowding in" or not. The second issue is the relative efficiency of state sector investments. This needs a lot of empirical research and, given the lack of hard data, any research on this topic is going to involve the value judgments of the researchers.

What Role, If Any, Does China's State Sector Play in the Imbalances of the Economy?

It is commonly agreed that the Chinese economy is "unsteady, imbalanced, and unsustainable," as Premier Wen Jiabao famously said in 2010 and which was repeated by thousands of others ever since then. One of the symptoms of the imbalances is that the economy is propped up by artificially high investments and still higher savings.

There is no dispute on this assessment. But what role has the dominant state sector played in the formation and continuation of the imbalances?

The root causes of the imbalances are:

- Depressed interest rates. This has encouraged the household sector to save more than it would otherwise. It has also encouraged the state sector to invest more, as lower hurdle rates make low quality opportunities seem feasible.
- Depressed local currency. That also effectively reduces the real income of the household sector.
- A weak social security system. That has had the effect of forcing people to save more than they would otherwise.

But is the dominance of the state sector a contributor to this process? Or, is it just a product of the same policies?

From an almost classless society in the 1950s through the 1980s, China has now become a country with extreme disparity. How did we get here in a short space of two to three decades? My view is that the state sector and official policies have been the major culprits. However, since we are here, rightly or wrongly the public seems to demand that the government and the state sector help undo the damage.

Between the 1950s and the 1980s, China was a very egalitarian though authoritarian society. For example, when I was at the central bank in Beijing in the 1980s, my salary was 52 yuan a month, compared to 35 to 45 yuan for SOE workers across the country. Most peasant farmers would make 20 yuan a month. Even ministers only made a monthly wage of 100 to 140 yuan a month. There was no visible elite class, and income disparity was modest.

Starting from the early 1990s, however, three factors dramatically and ruthlessly widened income gaps and wealth gaps.

1. Hundreds of thousands, possibly millions, of private entrepreneurs made their fortunes from their business ventures. They have not only contributed to the economic miracle of China, but also benefited from it. When nominal GDP compounded at around 15% to 16% a year for two or three decades, you know the scary outcome at the end of it. Contained in that nominal GDP growth was real growth plus inflation. But inflation benefits asset owners disproportionately. When they took out bank loans, they received a substantial subsidy as the interest rate was often below the inflation rate.

   These people were in the right place at the right time. They included restaurateurs, butchers, plantation owners, builders, taxi drivers, tailors, hairdressers, and a wide range of other new entrepreneurs. Unlike the tycoons in the post-Soviet Union era, these Chinese entrepreneurs made their fortunes primarily by putting in long hours, enduring hardships, and being creative and resourceful. Many of them took over failing SOEs and turned them around. When their profits were compounded for two or three decades, the end results are indeed impressive. Of my relatives, friends, fellow villagers, and former colleagues at the central bank, a large number made it this way. Their wealth is now in the range of a few million to hundreds of millions in U.S. dollars equivalent. In comparison, the more cautious people who have played it safe and stayed as employees in the civil service or SOEs are now significantly poorer.

To this social class, the Chinese public has mixed feelings: respect, envy, and sour grapes.

2. The second class of wealthy people is made up of corrupt officials. Their ranks are surprisingly large and they often fuel social discontent. It is this class that the new government is now targeting. In November 2013 alone, after the Communist Party's Third Plenum, a handful of minister-level officials were arrested for corruption. It is the consensus view that corruption is so deeply rooted that a political campaign alone is unlikely to change the landscape unless the state sector is substantially curtailed, along with a scaling back of government regulation in the economy. Unfortunately, that is not what the public wants to see. The public has not given up hope on the state sector or the government and, indeed, it wants the state sector and the government to help clean up the mess. Short of democratic checks and balances, the Internet and media are providing much-needed scrutiny.

3. The interest rate controls contributed to this inequality. For most of the past 35 years, interest rates have often been below inflation, and access to credit has been a windfall. Low interest rates effectively rip off the ordinary depositors to subsidize those borrowers.

Many officials understand this consequence, but are reluctant to change the status quo. And why not? They fear that the higher interest rates may push many businesses over the edge, and so attract hot money inflows which in turn will add to the pressure for the yuan to strengthen.

4. The rapid growth of money and credit and asset price inflation created a class of wealthy people who either controlled land, or speculated on real estate. In the past decade alone, the real estate prices across China have risen almost four-fold, and in capital cities, the surge has been more substantial.

5. The stock market contributed to the inequality. Insider trading was also a factor. But more importantly, the flawed regulations were the biggest factor. Since 1992, when the stock market was created, the government has kept tight controls on who was allowed to go public, when, and at what price. This has caused the stock prices to be excessively high in the early years of the market. As the supply of stocks increased over time, stock valuations started to decline, but limited supplies still meant that the prices were high. That managed process created millions of rich people who did not deserve their fortunes. Moreover, forged accounts and corporate thieves made things worse as well.

As you can see, inequality has largely been a byproduct, or accidental result, of the government's misguided policies of the past two to three decades. But since we have contracted the disease of inequality, we have to count on the government's visible hand to cure the disease. Or so the public believes.

Are the Current Economic Imbalances Sustainable?

The "Rebalancing School of Thought" has dominated much of the China debate inside and outside of China in recent years. The common conclusion is that the imbalances in China are so severe that they will lead to a collapse of economic activity, or a depression, in two to three years. The representative of this camp is Michael Pettis of Beijing University.

But there are two issues here. First, given the definitional issues and data discrepancies, there are scholars who doubt that China's savings and investments are as high as official data suggests. In a *Financial Times* piece, David Pilling noted that Jun Zhang and Tian Zhu, of Fudan University and China Europe International Business School, respectively, have argued that consumption has been consistently underreported. The pair estimates that China underestimates consumption by 10 to 12 percentage points.

Second, many in the "Rebalancing School of Thought" warn that China risks a collapse if household consumption rises from 34% of GDP to 50% in 10 years.

Mathematically, they are right. But why does China have to increase household consumption as a percentage of GDP from the current 34% to 50% in 10 years? That's the question. What will be the trigger for the current growth model to collapse? A bursting of the housing market bubble? But that, in itself, would not force consumption to become a more significant component of GDP.

To many savers, purchases of houses — particularly of multiple housing units — amount to spent household savings. As there is no clear place for people to invest their savings, housing purchases have become a default option for many. Though the people are aware of the possibility of their savings being wiped out in a housing bust, they are comforted by the fact that their leverage ratio is low.

Do China's 35 years of rapid growth represent a victory of Keynesian economics?

The official numbers presented earlier in the book showed that monetary policy has been very expansionary in the past 35 years. Broad money supply has grown at a compound annual rate of 21.1% in the 26 years from 1986 to 2012 [refer to page 100 of my book *Inside China's Shadow Banking: The Next Subprime Crisis?*]. In the long term, inflation should neutralize the benefits of monetary growth on economic activities. Has this been proven true in the past 35 years in China?

16
Chapter

A Way Forward?
Muddling Through

PARTY MAN, COMPANY MAN

If you were a *New China* watcher, you could be forgiven for getting excited at the policy documents that were announced after the closing of the Third Plenum of the Chinese Communist Party in November 2013. In fact, excitement was exactly the reaction of many Western observers in November.

I must confess that I had been caught by surprise when the stock market in Hong Kong reacted very positively to the policy documents. Numerous Western media outlets, from the *Financial Times* to *The Wall Street Journal*, and *The New York Times*, immediately published lengthy analysis pieces which offered predictions of transformational changes in China. Even experienced China observers such as Nicholas Lardy of the Peterson Institute for International Economics wrote enthusiastically on the government reform agenda in China.

Initially, the China economists at foreign banks in Hong Kong — economists who are mostly local Chinese — were lukewarm about the Third Plenum and the policy documents. But when they saw overwhelmingly positive reactions from the West, they started to revise their positions and hedge their bets. Reluctantly, they too wrote positive praise for the reforms. Then I forced myself to take a closer look at the policy documents and was convinced that the policy pronouncement this time was no different from the one made a year ago, or the ones made two, three, and four years ago.

Chinese politicians are good at making grand statements. The blueprint they released and their candid self-criticism is always heartwarming to the unaware. But few politicians have been as direct and blunt as former Premier Wen Jiabao in blasting the way that the Chinese economy has been managed. It's worth recalling his trademark criticism that the Chinese economy was "imbalanced, unstable, and unhealthy." Mr. Wen's statement of reform intention was also the most impressive to New China observers.

The only trouble with this is that China moves slowly,

especially slowly when it comes to reforms.

What reforms are necessary for China? I think China should immediately embark on at least the following:

1. Significantly reduce the size of the state sector in order to make way for the private sector;
2. Reduce the regulatory shackles on business, and reduce the ranks of civil servants;
3. Reduce distortions to prices including the prices of money (i.e., interest rates and exchange rates), and the prices of electricity, water, and gas; and
4. Spend money to clean up the environment, and create incentives for everyone to become a conservationist.

Sadly, I cannot honestly predict that these reforms will take place in the next few years. Indeed, I cannot predict if these reforms will be carried out ever.

Across China, I see the popular sentiment in favor of a bigger state sector and a stronger government. After their visits to India, many Chinese officials and members of the public have written in unison in official media outlets or the Internet about the need for a stronger government and a bigger state sector. Yang Zaiping, Secretary-General of the China Finance Association, was but a representative example of the blasting of the public failure in India. While they are openly critical of the inefficiency and corruption in China's state sector, the officials draw comfort from China's contrasts with India — on infrastructure, education, and the provision of essential public services. The fact that India is the biggest democracy in the world has not made the Chinese envious — although both countries face many of the same challenges such as red tape, corruption, and overpopulation. Note that these visitors are not just Chinese officials but also ordinary members of the public. When discussing India's younger demographic profile and China's aging population, one Chinese official who had recently returned from India expressed grave concerns about India's looming jobless crisis that made China's situation seem more manageable.

By the same token, the failure of a large number of free market democracies such as the Philippines, Thailand, and certain African countries to lift their populations out of poverty has given the Chinese a strong reason to lean towards a strong state sector, albeit not their own centrally-planned economy of the 1950s through the 1980s.

A Very Chinese Contradiction

One example best illustrates the contradiction in the attitude of the ordinary Chinese towards the establishment, the state sector, and the government. A few years earlier, e-commerce operators had cleverly turned Chinese Bachelors' Day on November 11 into a giant e-commerce day. On November 11, 2013, e-commerce transactions were said to exceed 35 billion yuan in total!

But why rush to order T-shirts, socks, books, or mobile phones on the Internet just because it was November 11? Are the prices cheaper on that day? Not necessarily. Some online merchants marked up the prices of the products on that day and then offered an eye-popping 25% discount. Millions of ordinary consumers knew that. But it was not the bargain that lured them to shopping on that particular day. Many consumers delayed their normal online purchases just for that day. On that day, they even ordered things they did not want or need. Millions were just excited to watch the game. Many people treated the tally of e-commerce transactions as a game, a match, a festivity, and a religious event. The media sensation was also unusual.

The e-commerce sector has become the poster child of the anti-establishment movement in China. It is where the tedious rules and red tape imposed by the old guard are either nonexistent or tolerable. The public's love affair with e-commerce is a declaration of their disdain with the establishment, the state sector, and the government. But the very same people also do whatever they can to get a job in the civil service or SOEs, trust the services by SOEs and the state sector more than the private sector, and demand a bigger state sector and tougher regulations. They also derive satisfaction from private entrepreneurs' falls from grace. Chinese websites and the large number of business magazines love to repeat the stories tirelessly of e-commerce entrepreneurs going bust, or losing money.

China's Habit of Policy Inaction

In no other language are there more ways of saying "doing nothing." In English, I can only find a few such phrases that do the trick like, "Kicking the can down the road." In Chinese, however, there are countless ways of saying these things, some of which even honor that attitude. For example, there is *"wuwei erzhi* 無為而治*"* (meaning that a true statesman should manage the country by doing nothing). A Chinese Buddhist approach to challenges is *"liaoyou weiliao* 了猶未了*"* which means that tackling a challenge is no better than leaving it alone. Another celebrated Chinese phrase for doing nothing, dragging on, or muddling through is *"weiwen* 維穩*"* which means "keeping social stability."

I see plenty of this muddling through in Chinese policies. Just because most people or even everyone agrees that something *must* be done does not mean that something *will* be done.

A case in point: Most observers agree that China's currency is undervalued and that the government has deliberately pursued a policy of currency undervaluation. But I disagree with that assessment. I think the undervaluation of the yuan is a typical example of the Chinese muddling through. Whatever the exchange rate happens to be, the tendency of the Chinese is to keep it as it is, even when it is a wrong rate (undervalued or overvalued).

PARTY MAN, COMPANY MAN

Suppose when we wake up tomorrow that the yuan is suddenly half its current value against the U.S. dollar (i.e., 12 yuan to 1 U.S. dollar instead of the current 6 yuan to the dollar). Do you think that the Chinese government and the public will be happier? No. That rate would be seen as too good or too favorable! They do not want something that is too good or too favorable. They will still want the old rate back, that is, 6 yuan to 1 U.S. dollar. If the market slowly moves toward 5 yuan to the dollar, then 5 will become the appropriate rate.

Today, the yuan's undervaluation is the result of many accidents, including China's higher productivity growth, its rapid build-up of an industrial base, and the erosion of purchasing power in other currencies.

Where China is wrong is its failure to take any policy action to reflect these accidents in its exchange rate policy. In other words, its fault lies in having done nothing instead of having done something proactive. What should China do about its currency? Liberalize the currency, or at least allow the yuan to appreciate more. Sadly, that is not the Chinese approach to policies.

The second example is the real estate bubble. Since 2007, the Mainland government has regularly pledged to bring down property prices and tame construction activity. However, the property bubble keeps getting bigger. The government knows the reasons behind the bubble — negative real interest rates and the low cost of holding on to real estate — but it does not want to address the real issues.

In 2010, the Chinese government announced a pilot scheme to introduce a property tax in Chongqing and Shanghai, and vowed to liberalize interest rates. Three years on, however, very little, if any, progress has been made on either front, apart from more vows and more frank words from senior officials. The document from the Communist Party's Third Plenum repeated the vow, but more vaguely and less forcefully than before.

On a related front, the government claims to be very

concerned about the proliferation of shadow banking activities, but it refuses to do what's necessary to tame shadow banking. And what is that? Higher interest rates. I reckon that if the commercial banks were allowed to raise interest rates on deposits by 2 percentage points, shadow banking will lose much of its appeal, and wealth management products will be down by half.

A quarter of a century ago, the central bank made it a goal to liberalize interest rates in five to seven years. But today, the central bank is still only tinkering around the edges.

There are many other examples of policy inaction. Despite terrible pollution, China's water wastage is widespread, as tariffs are far too low. Relative to income growth or inflation, water tariffs have declined in the past 10 years.

Another example: to reduce oil consumption, the government tabled a fuel tax bill 10 years ago, but a civilized debate in Congress killed it. Today, no one even talks about the fuel tax. The electricity price is far too low, but who dares raise it to its true economic value?

Do not underestimate the Chinese ability to muddle through.

17
Chapter

State Capitalism Works: My Open Letter to President Xi Jinping

Dear President Xi,

As your loyal subject, I have recently analyzed the Chinese economy, having worked for the central bank and several SOEs as well as the private sector. I humbly offer four pieces of advice to you.

1. Stay the course on state capitalism

Please stay the course on state capitalism, but leave growing room for the private sector. Do not indulge in wholesale privatization like what our Soviet friends did in the 1990s, and what the British did under Margret Thatcher a little earlier.

The reason why wholesale privatization can be harmful is twofold. Any country's choice of state capitalism or private sector capitalism has to consider the political, social, and cultural backdrop of that country. Moreover, private sector capitalism is not without problems, judging from the recent global crisis in the United States, and then in Europe, and the failure of many poor countries that have pinned unrealistic hopes on the "invisible hand" of the market.

Please allow me to elaborate on these two factors.

We Chinese have practiced communism, state ownership, and central planning since 1949. That's 64 years of accumulated experience. Therefore, the public and the bureaucrats need more time to gradually embrace something as fierce as private sector capitalism. True, we have liberalized the economy somewhat in the recent three decades, but this episode is associated with a lot of pains: a large portion of the population has been left behind, and there is now considerably more inequality than at any time in the past 64 years.

You know better than I do why China became a Communist state in 1949 and why the Nationalist KMT was thrown out of office and kicked out to Taiwan. Your father was a Communist leader and my grandfather was a Nationalist KMT member. But under the KMT's reign, capitalism quickly degenerated into a brutal type of feudal capitalism where democracy was only the veil for a money-grab by the few. That soon fuelled discontent, and despite the KMT's position as the government with all the resources that they needed at their fingertips, the KMT was overthrown by the Communists. The determining factor of that revolution was public support: The Communists had it, while the KMT did not. So, it is fair to say that Communism was the choice of the Chinese public in the 1940s.

Due largely to ideological fundamentalism and intolerance, the West (for all their talk of supporting freedom of choice) refuses to accept the choice the Chinese majority has made. Ignore them. We do not live to gain their endorsement. The bloody revolution of eight years (the Civil War against the Nationalist KMT which ended in 1949) was tougher and more revealing than any referendum we will see in the West. The Chinese public made a resounding statement with their sweat, blood, and lives. It is ludicrous that some Western observers describe the Communist regime or state capitalism as some sort of historical accident, a historical aberration, or just an odd occurrence.

I guess what I am saying is that state ownership of virtually every part of the economy has had its political, social, and cultural underpinning in China. Outsiders refuse to understand this, and preach to us on what we ought to choose in a condescending manner. I do not accept that, and I am sure most Chinese do not accept that.

All said, we Chinese are normally pragmatic and are willing to face reality and even acknowledge inconvenient truths. For example, in the past few hundred years, China has lagged far behind the West. But it would be unfair to blame our backwardness on Communism or state capitalism, as state pre-eminence in the economy has lasted only 64 years. Clearly, it is other and probably more fundamental factors that have held China back.

Neither private sector capitalism (the free market) nor state capitalism can guarantee economic development and the well-being of the citizenry. There are plenty of examples around the world to support this argument. In other places, many other factors are also at work. Of the poor countries in Africa, Asia, and Latin America, many have practiced free market capitalism and have not succeeded in lifting their citizens out of poverty. Admittedly, the track record of state capitalism since World War II has been much poorer. But who knows? China may become a notable exception some time down the road. Ha-Joon Chang of Cambridge University argues that Korea, Japan, and Singapore are all triumphs of state capitalism. Indeed, many other countries (including France and a few Scandinavian countries) are all practicing variations on state capitalism with success.

Even if free market capitalism is superior to state capitalism in the long term —as I suspect it is — it does not mean that China should take the plunge into capitalism without carefully considering its own cultural, political, and social background, and without a measured pace.

2. Persevere on the fight against corruption

Please continue the anti-corruption campaign you started after becoming President in March 2013. This effort is absolutely necessary and long overdue. Sadly, corruption is now endemic not only in the public sector, but also in the private sector. Indeed, it is much worse in the private sector. Tax evasion and all sorts of frauds are pervasive, but nowhere is it as bad as in the stock market and the real estate market. I feel that these are the two major sources of rising inequality. The government's ill-advised policies should take much of the blame. In 1949, the Nationalist KMT Party lost power due in part to a total loss of confidence by the public. We must heed that lesson.

You command tremendous respect and credibility among the Chinese public. I am a big fan, and a true believer in your policies.

3. Continue population control

Please continue population control. In my humble view, China has done a good job at slowing its population growth. Hannah Beech of *Time* magazine wrote on November 21, 2013, that China "will soon have too few people — or, rather, too few of the right kind of people." I do not buy her argument, and I also ask you not to.

Let's be honest about it: some aspects of China's population policy may be flawed, and the implementation at the grassroots levels is sometimes inhumane and brutal. These methods are wrong and have been criticized rightly by observers both at home and abroad. Our government must acknowledge those issues and correct the errors.

However, the idea of population control undoubtedly makes sense. I think it is more inhumane and brutal to have an overpopulated planet that is unable to provide the population with very basic services like water, food, clean air, and shelter.

China shares many similarities with neighboring India, Bangladesh, and Pakistan: we are all very poor, overpopulated, facing terrible environmental degradation, and suffering unbearable bureaucracy and corruption.

I recently read a brilliant book, *Reimagining India: Unlocking the Potential of Asia's Next Superpower*, edited by McKinsey & Company Inc., the consultancy firm. It is a collection of essays about what the 60-plus contributors think India should do to approach its full potential.

Victor Mallet, chief of the South Asia Bureau of *Financial Times*, contributed an excellent essay to the book. He gave a few sad facts in his essay, including that over 600 million Indians defecate in the open. But the libertarian and freedom of choice camp does not appear to accept the thesis that poverty is often a result of overpopulation. Mallet asked the obvious question: Is the world benefiting from a demographic dividend, or heading for a demographic disaster?

Mallet further challenged those who claim that India is capable of hosting a much larger population. "But this is the wrong question. They should be asking not whether it is possible but whether it is desirable for the world greatly to increase its population beyond the level of nine to ten billion or so it is already almost certain to reach."

Mallet quoted Paul R. Ehrlich's work, *The Population Bomb*, written while the author was living in Dehli 46 years ago when the Indian population was "merely" 500 million — less than half the current level! Ehrlich wrote the following: "People eating, people washing, people sleeping. People visiting, people arguing, and people screaming. People thrusting their hands through the taxi window, begging. People defecating and urinating. People clinging to buses. People herding animals. People, people, people."

Indeed, Ehrlich could have written that passage in China. As I asserted in my book, I believe the vast majority of the Chinese people support a sensible population policy, and a much smaller population. Compared to the many bad scenarios people have tried to scare us with, such as an aging society and a dwindling labor force, the current state of the planet is worse, in my view.

4. Deflate the asset bubble

Since 1978, China has indulged itself in an unprecedented inflationary policy. That might have contributed to economic growth by monetizing our old command economy, but it is now grossly overdone. Today's money supply is 372% of that at the beginning of 2006 — equivalent to a 17.8% compound annual growth rate. This is far more aggressive than the quantitative easing in the United States or Europe.

Now the high debts of China's corporate sector and the local governments are causing investors at home and abroad a lot of anxieties. It is the government sector — including SOEs — that has caused many of these problems. How? They are too insensitive to interest rates, and have an unlimited appetite for leverage and a low hurdle rate of returns. Their insatiable demand for credit and the government banks' unlimited appetite for bigger portfolios have reinforced each other, and have led to the credit explosion which we are now in. It requires a huge amount of skill to reduce leverage without killing the economy.

I have no good advice on this deleveraging process. But first and foremost, we must stop the credit explosion from getting worse. For example, the 13.6% growth rate in broad money supply as of the end of 2013 was simply too high on an already high base of a year earlier.

To bring the credit expansion under control, it will be a good idea to allow interest rates to float to reflect the true cost of money.

I understand that, as profit-maximizing business enterprises, SOEs are always going to be unnatural to some extent. So, the Chinese economy currently dominated by SOEs is an interim state of affairs. Eventually, say, in the next 50 to 100 years, China may well evolve into more of a free market with capitalism similar to what is in the U.S. today.

But there is no rush. One hundred years is just a blip in the many, many eras of China's long civilization. More haste, less speed.

Long live China!

Sincerely,
Joe Zhang
April 2014

Appendix

A Critique of the State Sector: My Conversation with an SOE Manager

Zhao Rong is Executive Directive and Vice President of a state-controlled infrastructure company listed on the Shenzhen Stock Exchange. He was one of my fellow directors at another SOE from 2006 to 2008. A long-time outspoken critic of the state sector, his views are widely known and shared by many. I do not entirely disagree with him; but just because you don't like something doesn't mean that you can make it disappear. In writing this book, I met with Zhao to pick his brains.

Zhang: What is the outlook of the state sector in general?

Zhao: I'm very bearish. Our corporate leaders are political appointees, not products of meritocracy, nor products of the battlefield. The troops are demoralized.

Zhang: But that's nothing new.

Zhao: True. But I am sick of seeing the game of musical chairs every three to five years. There is no continuity in management or strategy.

Zhang: But there are now more, not less, checks and balances than 5 or 10 years ago.

Zhao: Maybe. But you still see so much corruption everywhere.

Zhang: Is that because corruption is rising or because there is more scrutiny?

Zhao: Each year, a large number of SOEs are punished for corruption. But the checks and balances remain patchy. I don't know. Maybe both?

Zhang: How is your warehousing division doing these days?

Zhao: It generates a net profit of 100 million yuan on an equity base of 300 million yuan. On paper, that is a return of 33%. But we really should be selling the warehouse for redevelopment as the site is now almost at the center of a sprawling city. I think we can sell the site for as much as 4 billion yuan. On that basis, our current return from the warehouse is merely 2.5%. That's the way to look at things. But our chairman and president do not have a clue about business.

Zhang: But it is your job to explain these things to them and to promote change.

Zhao: No, no. I am just an employee. If I push too hard, the bosses may think I have some hidden agenda.

Zhang: I know that Sarah, your fiancée, now works for the big state-owned shipping group. What's the impact of the recent scandals (financial embezzlement involving senior executives) over there?

Zhao: No one is surprised about widespread corruption there. The corporate executives have too much power. No one is watching over their shoulders. The control mechanism was lax. But the crackdown may have unintended consequences: the group sits on billions of dollars of idle cash. No one is doing anything to increase the returns for shareholders.

Zhang: How did they get into that trap?

Zhao: In the past few years, the group lost huge amounts of money speculating on oil futures, and then on the shipping index, and finally on financial derivatives. The culprits have been duly punished. But other executives did not want to make another mistake: the less you do, the fewer mistakes you will make. They play it safe. Sadly, the group is virtually at a standstill. Disappointed, lots of veterans have migrated to other countries.

Zhang: What do you think of the strict limit of stock options for SOE managers [imposed by SASAC on SOEs]?

Zhao: I support those restrictions. Some SOEs in the past have abused the stock options to enrich themselves. These executives usually held two positions: one at the listed company and one at the parent company. They gave themselves lots of stock options at the listed company, and acquired assets from the parent company at ridiculously low prices. While the executives made fortunes, taxpayers lost out. Moreover, these companies' operational capabilities have not improved as a result of the capital market gimmicks.

Zhang: Do senior executives have the right incentives to perform these days?

Zhao: They have some insufficient incentives. If they do a good job, they will soon be posted elsewhere as their political enemies will scramble for the gravy train. The new office-holder will be a political winner, so the business will suffer. Then a capable guy will have to be brought in to clean up the mess. And then a dummy will take over. So, the quality of management at SOEs will oscillate like this forever.

Zhang: How are the private-sector rivals doing?

Zhao: They struggle because it is an unfair competition.

Zhang: How are the revelations about the U.S. spy agencies going to affect the Chinese state sector?

Zhao: I do not have a particular view on that subject. Like everyone else in the world, I was shocked by the extent of the U.S. spying. I suspect the revelations will make the Chinese government more cautious about foreign companies' equipment.

Zhang: The total compensation at SOEs is much higher than in the private sector. Is that fair?

Zhao: Of course not. The chart below shows that the average wages at SOEs are the highest, followed by so-called collective enterprises, and then the private sector. But these figures grossly underestimate the true extent of the unfairness. Employees at SOEs have higher job security, better prospects for promotion, and considerable perks.

Average annual wages in China

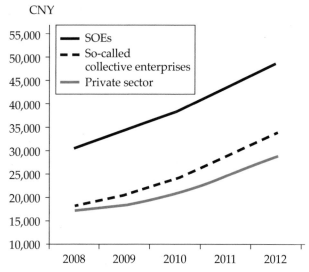

Source: National Bureau of Statistics, China

Zhang: But the compensation is increasingly linked to performance. Is that not a good thing?

Zhao: In principle, I support performance-linked compensation. But in practice, it is hard to implement. For example, China Mobile has much higher net profits per employee than, say, at a port handling facility. But is it fair for China Mobile to pay each of its employees millions of dollars? The banking industry benefits from officially-controlled interest rates. Therefore, the banks' financial results do not really reflect their operational efficiency. Finally, there is the trade-off between building long-term corporate value and taking short-term risks. The U.S. subprime crisis shows that a rigged compensation system can lead to excessive risk-taking.

Acknowledgements

From 2006 to 2008, I spent two and a half years at Shenzhen Investment Limited as its Chief Operating Officer. I thank the former Chairman, Hu Aimin, and Chief Executive Officer, Zhang Yijun, for giving me the opportunity. They taught me many tricks of navigating a bureaucratic government company.

Other things I learned while working at Shenzhen Investment Limited:

1. Predicting the state sector's demise because of its inefficiency and corruption is like shorting a stock just because it is expensive.
2. Libertarians have disdain about the state sector, but most members of the Chinese public do not share the same view.
3. It is condescending to judge other people's choices. Whether shoes are good or not, feet are the only judge.

My management style was aggressive. I thank my former colleagues for accommodating me, and forgiving me.

In those three years at Shenzhen Investment, I benefited tremendously from the professionalism and commitment of Kalvin Zhu (now Chief Operating Officer and then assistant to CEO), Lu Jiqiang (Head of Legal), Nicole Zhou (Manager of Investor Relations), Qiu Guizhong (Chief of Staff), and Chloe Wu (my assistant). We worked as a team, and I have taken much of the credit for their behind-the-scene contributions.

My editor at Enrich Professional Publishing, Glenn Griffith, has guided me on this book, and my previous book, *Inside China's*

Acknowledgements

Shadow Banking: The Next Subprime Crisis?. I owe him enormously for his patience, insights, and editorial work. Glenn has also edited most of my essays and op-eds in various newspapers and other outlets.

Vivian Hui at Enrich Professional Publishing worked tirelessly on this book's many revisions, and I thank her for her patience and efficiency.

About the Author

Joe Zhang, 51, is a corporate governance advisor based in Hong Kong.

He worked for 11 years at UBS, mainly as Head of China Research and then Deputy Head of its China Investment Banking Division.

From 1986 to 1989, he was an official of the central People's Bank of China in Beijing. From 2006 to 2008, he was the Chief Operating Officer of Shenzhen Investment Limited, a government company.

Joe received a Master of Economics degree from the Australian National University in 1991, and he was a lecturer of banking and finance at the University of Canberra from 1991 to 1994.

In the past two decades, his numerous articles have appeared in *The Wall Street Journal*, *Financial Times*, Bloomberg, *South China Morning Post*, *The Australian Financial Review*, *The New York Times*, and the *International Herald Tribune*. He published two best-selling Chinese books, *The Confessions of a Stock Analyst* (投行分析師的叛逆宣言) and *Avoiding Land Mines in the Stock Market* (避開股市的地雷).

In 2001, while an analyst, he wrote negative research on Greencool Technology and Euro-Asia. Greencool sued Joe in the Hong Kong High Court. Both companies have since gone belly-up and been delisted from the Hong Kong Stock Exchange. The chairmen of both companies eventually served long jail sentences.

email: joezhang88@yahoo.com
blog: www.blog.sina.com.cn/joezhang33

Selected Works of Joe Zhang

Books

Inside China's Shadow Banking: The Next Subprime Crisis?.
Honolulu: Enrich Professional Publishing, 2013.

避開股市的地雷 (Avoiding Land Mines in the Stock Market).
Hong Kong: Enrich Publishing, 2012.

投行分析師的叛逆宣言 (The Confessions of a Stock Analyst).
Hong Kong: Enrich Publishing, 2010.

Articles

The New York Times and International Herald Tribune:

"Smarter Management of Investment Inflow." July 9, 1996.

"There Goes Chinese Frugality." July 29, 1996.

"Refusing a Windfall at Doorstep." August 13, 1996.

"Don't Expect Chinese Wages to Go Up Any Time Soon." October 13, 1998.

"What Smuggling Did for China." November 23, 1998.

"When a Brother in China Calls to Ask for Money." December 1, 2000.

"A Return Home to China Is Now a Worrying Trip." February 22, 2001.

"Harsh Reality of China's Divide." May 3, 2001.

"China's Coming Wave of Privatization." August 13, 2013.

Selected Works of Joe Zhang

Financial Times:

"China's Private Sector in the Shadow of the State." October 4, 2005.

"Rising Rates Will Help Cure China's Credit Addiction." January 12, 2014.

Bloomberg:

"Why I Became a Chinese Shadow Banker." July 9, 2013.

Reuters:

"China's Shadow Banks Deserve Credit." July 8, 2013.

"Why China's Bad Banks Are a Bad Idea." October 16, 2013.

The Economist:

"Reasons to be Bullish on Chinese Banks." September 13, 2013.

South China Morning Post:

"The Real Problem Behind China's Shadow Banking." May 31, 2013.

"Time to Pour Cold Water on Hot Money." July 2, 2013.

"Why Chinese Stocks Perform Poorly." July 27, 2013.

"The Quick Buck Economy." September 24, 2013.

"Time to Pull the Trigger." October 8, 2013.

"Lending in the Shadows." October 24, 2013.

"Bank On the Banks." November 9, 2013.

"Why a Recession Would Be Good for China." January 24, 2014.

Bibliography

Beech, Hannah. "China, the World's Most Populous Nation, Needs More Children." *Time*, November 21, 2013.

Bremmer, Ian. *The End of the Free Market: Who Wins the War Between States and Corporations?* New York: Portfolio, 2010.

Buffett, Warren, and Carol Loomis. "Warren Buffett On The Stock Market." *Fortune*, December 10, 2001.

Burrough, Bryan, and John Helyar. *Barbarians at the Gate: The Fall of RJR Nabisco*. New York: Harper & Row, 1990.

Chang, Gordon G. *The Coming Collapse of China*. New York: Random House, 2001.

Chang, Ha-Joon. *23 Things They Don't Tell You About Capitalism*. London: Penguin, 2010.

Eberstadt, Nicholas. "China's Coming One-Child Crisis." *The Wall Street Journal*, November 26, 2013.

Ehrlich, Paul R. *The Population Bomb*. New York: Ballantine Books, 1971.

Lardy, Nicholas R. *Sustaining China's Economic Growth After the Global Financial Crisis*. Washington, DC: Peterson Institute for International Economics, 2012.

Mazzucato, Mariana. *The Entrepreneurial State: Debunking Public vs. Private Sector Myths*. London: Anthem Press, 2013.

McKinsey & Company Inc., ed. *Reimagining India: Unlocking the Potential of Asia's Next Superpower*. New York: Simon & Schuster, 2013.

Nair, Chandran. *Consumptionnomics: Asia's Role in Reshaping Capitalism and Saving the Planet*. Oxford: Infinite Ideas, 2011.

Bibliography

Pilling, David. "China May Be In Much Better Shape Than It Looks." *Financial Times*, October 16, 2013.

Rey, Hélène. "Big Idea: Control Capital Flows." *Financial Times*, November 29, 2013.

Wooldridge, Adrian. "State Capitalism: The Visible Hand." *The Economist*, January 21, 2012.

Zhang, Joe. "China's Private Sector in Shadow of the State." *Financial Times*, October 4, 2005.

———. *Inside China's Shadow Banking: The Next Subprime Crisis?*. Honolulu: Enrich Professional Publishing, 2013.

Index